LEAD
with
Humility

---

12 LEADERSHIP LESSONS FROM POPE FRANCIS

Jeffrey A. Krames

HARPERCOLLINS
LEADERSHIP

AN IMPRINT OF HARPERCOLLINS

Lead with Humility

© 2015 Jeffrey A. Krames

Published by HarperCollins Leadership, an imprint of HarperCollins Focus LLC.

Any internet addresses, phone numbers, or company or product information printed in this book are offered as a resource and are not intended in any way to be or to imply an endorsement by HarperCollins Leadership, nor does HarperCollins Leadership vouch for the existence, content, or services of these sites, phone numbers, companies, or products beyond the life of this book.

Bulk discounts available. For details visit:
www.harpercollinsleadership.com/bulkquotes
Email: customercare@harpercollins.com

ISBN 978-0-8144-4911-0 (HC)
ISBN 978-1-4002-4558-1 (paperback)

This book is dedicated to my mother,
Trudy Krames (1933–2012);
my father, Barton "Baruch" Krames;
my amazing wife, Nancy;
and my incredible sons,
Noah Sidney and Joshua Michael.

These five souls have helped me to feel
closer to Pope Francis every day.

Contents

Contents

Prologue

For me, this is not just another leadership book. It is a deeply personal one.

I am not a member of the Catholic Church. I am not even a Christian. I am the son of Holocaust survivors: My father was born in Poland and lost every member of his family to the Third Reich. His story is so incredible that it was recorded by Steven Spielberg's Shoah Foundation—the digital remembrance the famed director created after making *Schindler's List.*

My mother—born Jewish in Frankfurt—was orphaned when she was shipped to England with thousands of other children on the Kindertransport that began in late 1938.

I have never mentioned any of this in any of the other books I have written. It would not have been appropriate or pertinent in any other book. But I do so here, in this book about the leadership of Pope Francis, because my motivation for writing this book is informed, in large part, by my own lot in life as the son of Holocaust survivors.

My parents, both members of highly religious Jewish families, were deeply affected by Hitler's killing machine. For them, World War II never ended. They had to live with the horrific losses and the inhumane atrocities they witnessed and endured.

Countless studies have been done on the effects of the Holocaust on subsequent generations of survivors. For me, it meant that I was afraid to leave the small Bronx apartment I grew up in—afraid that it was not safe to venture far from home for fear of the dangers that lurked outside. I picked that up from my father, Baruch Krames, who trusted no one during his unlikely—though ultimately successful—two-year run from the Nazis.

During that time, he lived like an animal in the woods, but that did not stop him from stealing food from the rich in order to bring it back to people starving in the Jewish ghetto.

What my father experienced—and witnessed—has stayed with him for a lifetime. He witnessed his brother being shot as he and his older brothers ran from Nazi troops. He also witnessed, on more than one occasion, hundreds of dead Jews lying one atop the other on the back of large German flatbed military trucks like so many bricks piled high at some construction site. I, of course, witnessed no such things, but they are no less etched in my mind.

Worst of all, the teenage Baruch had to make a *Sophie's Choice*-like decision, leaving his younger brother on a train bound for Auschwitz as he escaped through a small hole in the wall of the train, a hole that other Jews used to gasp for a rare breath of air (and that was just one of three trains he escaped from, incredibly).

The Holocaust is a subject for another book; it is worth noting here, however, because I have always felt, very deeply and often not consciously, my parents' pain. It was like being born into a family of ghosts—the ghosts of all of the people my parents lost under Hitler. It is why I have always placed such great importance on the respect and dignity of others, and why I am particularly sensitive to those who violate what I believe to be such core elements of the character that defines me.

What does all of that have to do with a leadership book on Pope Francis?

Shortly after the white puff of smoke lingered over the Vatican in March 2013, signaling the elevation of a new pope, Francis emerged as the anti-Hitler—as someone who places enormous value on respect, dignity, and humanity in every shape, color, and form.

He is the twenty-first century's answer to the twentieth century's most malevolent mass murderer.

This excerpt from Pope Francis's best-known homily underscores the point: "Just as the commandment 'Thou shall not kill' sets a clear limit in order to safeguard the value of human life, today we also have to say 'thou shall not' to an economy of exclusion and inequality."

The numbers reveal the polar opposites that these two world leaders represent. Most everyone knows that Hitler killed more than six million Jews. What is less known is that during 2013, his first year in Rome, Pope Francis's events and masses were attended by more than six million people, with many of those new or returning to the Church.

Examples abound of the utter humility—and humanity—of Pope Francis. Before he became pope, Archbishop Jorge Mario Bergoglio would go out in the dark of night in Buenos Aires to offer help to poor people. Now, as pope, he has asked an archbishop to do this for him.

Prior to the conclave, before he was selected as pope, Bergoglio stayed at a modest local hostel.

During his presentation as the new pope, Francis chose not to stand on the customary platform as his predecessors have for generations. Instead he said, according to Cardinal Timothy Dolan, "I'll stay down here."

For his seventy-seventh birthday in December 2013, Pope Francis invited four homeless people to celebrate with him—not for a photo op, which is so common in high government, but because those are the people with whom the pope feels most comfortable.

During his first year as pope—as during his tenure in Argentina—Francis showed himself again and again to be a man of humility. However, we mustn't confuse his humble ways with those of a one-dimensional leader. Like all effective leaders, he has multiple agendas. In fact, according to the journalists who have covered Bergoglio for many years, he is nothing short of "a political animal." He is also a man of enormous intellect, which often gets obscured by his acts of humility.

"He was not an ingénue coming out into the world," said Elisabetta Piqué, an Argentine journalist who has known Bergoglio since the 1990s and whose book, *Francisco: Vida y Revolución* ("Francis: Life and Revolution"), describes the issue he has had with Rome. "He had almost a war with [one] section of the Roman Curia," asserted Piqué.

Another journalist used the word "ruthless" to describe the way Francis operates.

And *Rolling Stone* cover-story journalist Mark Binelli wrote, "Bergoglio has shown himself to be a stealth enforcer, capable of summoning that old authoritarian steel if it serves a higher purpose."

Pope Francis certainly is a shrewd operator, already ridding the Curia of the leaders he believes are most fixated on the ways of yesterday, those who might interfere with his agenda of creating a more inclusive and open Church focused on meeting the needs of all people.

It is no accident that one of Pope Francis's best-known books, *On Heaven and Earth*, was coauthored with a well-known Argentine rabbi, his friend Abraham Skorka. It is also no accident that the book promotes itself by discussing how Bergoglio and Skorka spent years "building bridges among Catholicism, Judaism, and the world at large."

For example, as pope, Francis challenges the ultraconservatives in the Church to be ultrainclusive of people whom other popes never bothered to embrace: He washes the feet of prisoners (including two women, which caused no small amount of controversy with Church elders; no pope had washed the feet of women); he also embraces a man with boils whom few of us would ever approach, never mind embrace.

It should come as no surprise that Pope Francis despises waste and displays of great wealth, especially among members of the clergy, and he backs that sentiment with action. In late 2013, Pope Francis (temporarily) "expelled" a German bishop because he had the gall to spend an astronomical €31 million to erect a new, ostentatious home. An investigation was ordered to determine the ultimate future of the bishop labeled the "bling bishop." By the end of March 2014, The German "bling bishop" was removed from his diocese permanently.

Pope Francis sees no place in the Church for such spendthrifts, especially when so many in the world are in so much need. Indeed, it is this quote from Pope Francis that embodies his view of the world:

How can it be that it is not a news item when an elderly homeless person dies of exposure, but it is news when the stock market loses two points?

That's him—in a single sentence. Pope Francis shows us where the world has gone wrong and how our values have gone off the rails. Even the choice of his name—inspired by St. Francis of Assisi—was meant to signal to the world that he would focus on society's poor, as well as on the sickest and weakest among us.

Saint Francis of Assisi, who lived in the early part of the thirteenth century, became the patron saint of animals and ecology. Despite the fact that his father was wealthy, St. Francis gave up all that he once possessed, even his clothes, which he presented to his "earthly" father, all in an effort to follow the words of Jesus, who said: "Possess no gold or silver or copper in your purses, no traveling bag, no sandals, no staff." St. Francis of Assisi would likely approve of the contemporary Pope Francis.

However, Pope Francis's comment about the homeless and the Dow is a double-edged sword: In addition to revealing something important about Francis, it reveals the greatest challenge of writing a leadership book about this singular figure.

Francis has been criticized for his anticapitalistic tendencies. Although it might seem like semantics, Pope Francis is not anti-industry. He is, however, a harsh critic of large corporations that rack up billions in profits while laying off or firing thousands of workers: "The economy can no longer turn to remedies that are a new poison," wrote Francis, "such as attempting to increase profits by reducing the work force and thereby adding to the ranks of the excluded."

Why not interpret the pope's rhetoric as antibusiness? In the same homily in which he writes of the "excluded," he writes of the nobility of business and specifically of businesses that set out to make our world a better place to live: "Business is a vocation, and a noble vocation, provided that those engaged in it see themselves challenged by a greater meaning in life; this will enable them truly to serve the common good by striving to increase the goods of this world and to make them more accessible to all. . . . I am convinced of one thing: the great changes in history were realized when reality was seen not from the center but rather from the periphery."

So, despite all the pundits who have criticized Pope Francis for his antibusiness leanings, those criticisms are either simplistic or incomplete—and in some cases just wrong. However, Francis is certainly antigreed and, more to the point, anti–income inequality.

Pope Francis speaks eloquently on the topic of the underlying reasons for the increasingly pervasive problem of income inequality. "A new tyranny is thus born, invisible and often virtual, which unilaterally and relentlessly imposes its own laws and rules. . . . The thirst for power and possessions knows no limits. In this system, which tends to devour everything which stands in the way of increased profits, whatever is fragile, like the environment, is defenseless before the interests of a deified market, which becomes the only rule."

Denying the thirst for power and possessions is just one reason Pope Francis rebukes members of the clergy who drive new, expensive cars, urging them instead to buy used cars and donate the sticker-price difference to hungry, homeless children.

Pope Francis's desire to minister to the needy is certainly a goal with merit, and the pontiff has the statistics on his side to prove his point. In early 2014, Oxfam, the controversial antipoverty organization operating in more than ninety countries, revealed a near-unbelievable fact: The eighty-five richest people in the world have more money than all of the 3.5 billion poorest people on the planet combined. That means that the 1 percent of the richest people in the world control 46 percent—nearly half—of the world's wealth. With numbers like those, who could blame this pope for asking the wealthiest among us to give more?

However, that still doesn't diminish the difficulty of writing an authentic and helpful business book centered around a figure whose greatest goal is leveling the economic playing field. But this is not just a business book—it is a *leadership* book. And to make sure there is no confusion, this is the definition of leadership that will be employed throughout this book:

> *Leadership is the ability to articulate a vision and get others to carry it out.*

It is not without irony that this definition was originally espoused by the leader of one of the world's largest and oldest corporations, one who fired more than 125,000 workers: Jack Welch, former CEO of General Electric (who was named Manager of the Century by *Fortune* magazine and is the subject of several books I have authored).

Jack Welch and Pope Francis, while disagreeing fiercely on many things, would agree on some other important leadership tenets. For example, Welch liked to compare his $100 billion corporation to a corner grocery store. That is, he wanted all of his people to know both the products on their shelves and their customers intimately—certainly on a first-name basis.

Welch and Pope Francis also would agree on this important business principle: One of the hallmarks of any leader is how he or she leads by example. This is where Pope Francis shines. He leads a simpler life than perhaps any of his predecessors, driving what he calls a "modest" car—a Ford Focus. Before he was pope, he was known to take public transportation and lived in a small apartment in Buenos Aires. After he became pope, he had the papal throne removed from the Vatican and chose to live in a two-bedroom apartment rather than somewhere far more opulent. Francis lives by a set of values that consistently places others before himself, viewing his leadership role as a servant. "Let us never forget that authentic power is service," proclaimed Pope Francis during his inaugural mass. Service is a theme that runs like a thread throughout this book.

* * *

Before moving on, I should point out that I am not the first author to compare leadership in the Church with leadership in other institutions—such as corporations, nonprofits, or any other type of organization. One of the first was Peter Drucker, "the father of modern management."

I consider his 1946 book, *Concept of the Corporation*, based on the first large-scale study of a major corporation (General Motors), the grandfather of the modern-day business book, and many of the ideas in that book are still relevant today. Drucker wrote: "Any society needs institutions which by their very nature cannot be related to social goals. This is, for instance, true of the family which finds its purpose in the biological survival of man, and which is thus a condition of society rather than conditioned by it; and the same is true of a church whose kingdom is not of this world, and which therefore transcends society."

Drucker then added something that could have been written by Pope Francis: "If a social institution operates in such a manner as to make difficult or impossible the attainment of the basic ethical purposes of society it will bring about a severe political crisis. . . ." Drucker continued, ". . . What is often overlooked is that equality of opportunity and the human dignity of status and function stand in a very peculiar relationship to each other."

These sentiments are echoed by Pope Francis: "It is vital that government leaders and financial leaders take heed and broaden their horizons, working to ensure that all citizens have dignified work, education and healthcare."

Pope Francis also commented on the shifting of social structures: "Changing structures without generating new convictions and attitudes will only ensure that those same structures will become, sooner or later, corrupt, oppressive, and ineffectual."

In his book *Managing in a Time of Great Change,* Drucker also wrote about the changing ways of structures: "It is hard to fight them [structural trends] in the short-term and almost hopeless in the long-run. When such a structural trend peters out or when it reverses itself . . . those who continue as before face extinction." He continues, "[T]he tremendous increase in wealth-producing capacity . . . has been spent on greater leisure, on health care, and on education."

Here again is Pope Francis: "The renewal of structures demanded by pastoral conversion can only be understood in this light: as part of an effort to make them more mission-oriented, to make ordinary pastoral activity on every level more inclusive and open."

In early 2014, Francis urged global leaders gathered in Davos, Switzerland, to consider their broader roles in the world order: "I ask you to ensure humanity is served by wealth, and not ruled by it."

It is remarkable that many of Drucker's writings so closely resemble many of the thoughts and beliefs espoused by Pope Francis today. These figures share other similarities as well, many having to do with their humility: Both men are self-effacing, both lived well within their means, and both are superb thinkers. Even their writing styles—somewhat formal in nature—are similar.

In fact, having studied the vast majority of the great CEOs of the late twentieth century, I can think of no business leader who writes more thoughtfully about the global nature of business and wealth than Pope Francis. That is why his words—and actions—carry so much weight.

For example, when one takes into account the Great Recession of 2008–9, against the backdrop of a global crisis of increasing income inequality, it is difficult to argue with this statement made by the pope: "Some people continue to defend trickle-down theories which assume that economic growth, encouraged by a free market, will inevitably succeed in bringing about greater justice and inclusiveness in the world."

Francis may be a self-described "sinner"—to quote him, "[a] religious who recognizes himself as weak and a sinner does not negate the witness he is called to give, rather he reinforces it, and this is good for everyone"—but he is, without question, the right man for the right job at the right time. And the planets seldom align themselves as neatly as they have for this modest yet brilliant figure.

* * *

A note about the assumptions and approach I started with before writing this book: One assumption was that despite Pope Francis's predilection to fight against income inequality, his teachings—and, more important, his actions—have a great deal to offer anyone who aspires to lead others in any organization, regardless of size, type, environment, or situation.

The other key point is the approach of this book. Obviously this is a book *about* Pope Francis, not a book *by* Pope Francis. I am therefore responsible for its content. As such, it is important to note at the outset that this book represents my interpretation of the words and actions of Pope Francis.

In addition, I am no theologian or expert in Catholicism. My expertise is in leadership, as I have interviewed and studied many of the best business leaders of the last decades of the twentieth century as well as several of the twenty-first.

My view of Pope Francis differs from, say, that of a practicing member of the Catholic Church or a theologian; I see him through a more secular lens, and it is through such a lens that I can discern the many leadership principles that he lives by or preaches—or both. I certainly have been amazed by the unlikely route on which Francis is leading the Catholic religion in order to make it a more open, welcoming, and inclusive religion. For example, in late May 2014, Pope Francis told reporters on a papal plane ride back to Rome (after visiting the Middle East) that since celibacy is not dogma, "the door is always open." Throughout this book you will read about a great number of topics for which Francis "opens the door," including divorce and same-sex civil unions. It is these stunning pronouncements that have wreaked havoc with the far-right members of the Church but have simultaneously turned Bishop Bergoglio into Pope Francis, a journey that has been filled with acts of great humility, dignity, and courage.

From Bergoglio to Francis

S ince thousands packed St. Peter's Square in March 2013 for the inauguration of Pope Francis I, the Argentinian Jesuit has proven himself to be a pope like no pope before him. He has captured the attention of not only faithful Catholics but also lapsed Catholics, people from other denominations and religions, political leaders, media pundits, and so many others who have become enamored with this modest man.

Jorge Mario Bergoglio—the first non-European to be elevated to the papacy since 741 A.D.—was in many ways an unlikely successor to Pope Benedict XVI, surprising those who expected the conclave to select an Italian or an American or someone more outwardly conservative. Regardless, the choice to elevate Argentina's Provincial Superior of the Society of Jesus to Bishop of Rome and absolute Sovereign of the Vatican City State has pleased many different constituencies. In fact, shortly after *Time* magazine named Pope Francis its 2013 Person of the Year, an ABC/Washington Post poll found that "92 percent of Catholics express a favorable opinion of Pope Francis, 16 percentage points higher than those polled about Pope Benedict XVI" earlier that year.

What is it about this leader that has drawn the attention of so many? Perhaps it is the humility he displays both in how he lives his life and in how he leads his flock. Perhaps it is the genuine concern he shows for other people, regardless of their station in life. Perhaps it is in the way he embraces sincerity and austerity at a time when the Church has been lambasted for losing touch with its followers.

It's all of that and more. Pope Francis shows himself to be a leader who understands that leaders lead *people*, not institutions. Unfortunately, too few people understand this in an increasingly impersonal, high-tech working environment. We live in an age marred by a dearth of leadership. Today, fewer leaders roam the halls of our largest corporations, setting examples of positive, effective leadership. Unlike decades ago, many of us have never witnessed *authentic* leadership in action—until now, with the genuineness that we see every day from Pope Francis.

The vast majority of us have seldom, if ever, had a front-row seat to Francis-like leadership. But, just so there is no room for misunderstanding, this pope is not perfect. He consistently calls himself a "sinner" and does not demand perfection from anyone. "Who am I to judge" has become his most memorable "five words," reflecting more than mere tolerance when it comes to believers, nonbelievers, and even the most flawed among us. However, leadership is not about perfection; it is about espousing a new vision and getting others to live that vision. In that respect, Pope Francis has been incredibly successful. Peter Drucker would call him a "natural," a "born leader."

Every day, global media focus on some new act of leadership from Pope Francis. Whether calling the young author of a "beautifully written" letter to thank him for his kindness and to discuss his thoughts, whether conversing with some very surprised nuns on New Year's Eve and disrupting their celebration, or whether giving a ride to a friend in the popemobile, this humble, pious man demonstrates the kind of authenticity and hands-on approach that can inspire the rest of us to be great leaders. This is particularly noteworthy in an age when there doesn't seem to be a leader who can be counted on, from the Congressional offices to the corner office. That's why the time has come for *Leading with Humility*.

There is much to be learned from Pope Francis—and we will learn much more as his papacy unfolds. But in many ways we can already see the manner in which he demonstrates authentic leadership. We see how he looks for innovative ways to balance new realities while breaking free of a constrictive past. We see how he uses cold-calling techniques to communicate with all "employees." We see how he embraces all of God's creatures, including—and especially—the meekest and weakest among us, and creates an environment in which all can thrive. We see how he listens to and considers the thoughts and needs of others, finding ways to connect with those who have left the Church. And we can see how he considers all points of view, using discernment and counsel to make the best decisions, rather than making snap judgments on his own. This kind of genuine leadership is needed in today's world—as needed as it is rare.

A natural leader, Pope Francis I has enamored millions around the world—including me. Admittedly, I am not a Christian nor a theologian, yet this pope has moved me beyond words. He speaks to me in a way that no other global figure has. Instead of being afraid of change, he yearns for it. He is not afraid of shaking up the status quo. He is not afraid of disruptive innovation. These are among just a few of the hallmarks of a highly effective leader.

And Pope Francis is a great leader—a great leader who becomes more compelling by the day. Whether he is too progressive or too conservative will be decided by theologians and political pundits as well as millions of Catholics who will be following his every move for years to come. Whether he is an effective leader, however, is not debatable. Pope Francis has proven to be not only a man of the people but a leader among leaders. If he had been a leader in the business arena, he would rank right up there with leaders who built and transformed the organizations they led and/or founded: people like Bill Gates (Microsoft), Jack Welch (GE), Steve Jobs (Apple), Andy Grove (Intel), and Sam Walton (Walmart).

Aspiring leaders and students of leadership will find much to learn from this unique man, lessons that can be applied to all walks of life, but especially to business and, more specifically, leadership.

✦ Who Is Jorge Mario Bergoglio?

Although he likely would be the last to call himself a natural leader or a born leader—such self-praise would be completely out of character for a priest who came up in the Ignatian tradition—Pope Francis has, indeed, led a life marked by compassionate, effective leadership, although the Church was not his first calling.

As a young man, Jorge Mario Bergoglio (born December 17, 1936, in Buenos Aires) considered medicine as a profession, planning to become either a doctor or a pharmacy technician. But one summer day when he was 17, Bergoglio stopped by a church to make a confession. That day would prove a turning point for the teenager. He was so deeply moved by the priest who heard his confession that he changed his plans—not only for that day but also for his entire life. Bergoglio felt in that moment, with that priest, in that church, that God invited him to follow Him. And so he did.

After a few years working odd jobs, including stints as a nightclub bouncer, a janitor, a chemical technician, and a teacher of literature, Bergoglio entered Inmaculada Concepción Seminary, the archdiocesan seminary of Villa Devoto in Buenos Aires.

In March 1958, he entered the novitiate of the Society of Jesus, embarking on what would be a relatively long journey to priesthood:

It would be more than eleven years before Bergoglio was ordained a priest.

During the coming years, Father Bergoglio would study philosophy and theology, completing his tertianship (a period of strict discipline in the Jesuit order) and taking his perpetual vows in April 1973. He then served as provincial superior of the Society of Jesus in Argentina until 1979.

From 1980 to 1986, Father Bergoglio served as rector of the Philosophical and Theological Faculty of San Miguel—essentially the manager over all of Argentina's Jesuits. When that six-year term was over, Bergoglio's successor appointed him to a new position, as is tradition in the order. Bergoglio was assigned to mentor trainees in Córdoba. It was a step down—or at least that's how it would have looked on a résumé.

Again, Jorge Mario Bergoglio took what some would have seen as a disappointment in stride. Instead of viewing the new post as an unwelcome setback, he viewed it as an opportunity to learn more about the people he would be leading—and as an opportunity to learn more about himself and his relationship with God, considering the post simply yet another way to serve the Church rather than as a demotion.

Although many may have viewed such a step as a professional misstep, the position in no way blocked Bergoglio's path to Rome—not that a Vatican post was a position he aspired to. Such aspiration would not be in keeping with the Jesuit order, and, indeed, Pope Francis has admitted that being the Bishop of Rome was not exactly in his future. As he told students in June 2013, "No. I did not want to be pope. Is that okay?"

Nonetheless, Bergoglio's path was, indeed, one of an upward career trajectory. In 1992, he was named auxiliary bishop of Buenos Aires. Six years later, he became metropolitan archbishop of Buenos

Aires, where he created new parishes and restructured the administrative offices. In 2005, he was elected president of the Argentine Episcopal Conference; he was reelected to another three-year term in 2008 and then remained a member of the conference's permanent governing body.

By this time, Bergoglio was in his seventies; his work with the Church spanned the end of the twentieth century to the beginning of the twenty-first century. During those years, he had become known as a humble man, with a predilection for riding the bus to work, often seen in boots soiled from the dust and dirt of the farms on which he worked and the *barrios* where he visited the faithful as well as those who were not members of the Church. He had become recognized as a leader committed to open, respectful communication with all people from all walks of life, regardless of religion or politics.

In December 2011, however, he submitted his resignation to Pope Benedict XVI, as was required by Canon Law, which mandates that Catholic bishops resign their positions upon reaching their seventy-fifth birthdays. But a life of retirement was not to follow.

In March 2013, nearly fifty-three years to the day since Bergoglio officially became a Jesuit, he was elected by the conclave to be pope. Now, as Pope Francis, he leads 1.2 billion Catholics—and a Church racked by controversy and ripe for change. But it is certainly a task he is ready for, as foreshadowed by his unprecedented acts of leadership. For example, in late May 2014, during a trip to the Middle East, Pope Francis extended invitations to the presidents of Palestine and Israel to come to the Vatican "to pray." This took place only a few weeks after Middle East peace talks brokered by the United States collapsed. Both leaders accepted the invitation. Whether this will lead to something of substance remains to be seen; it is, however, one of dozens of unprecedented acts of leadership that you will read about in the twelve leadership lessons of Pope Francis that follow.

CHAPTER 1

Lead with Humility

Arecent *Harvard Business Review* blog post noted, "We have scores of books, articles, and studies that warn us of the perils of hubris . . ." and then added, pointedly, "Yet the attribute of humility seems to be neglected in leadership development programs." Perhaps this owes to some feeling that humility would hold a leader back, these mavericks and sui generis leaders who dislike being restrained. Some other leaders might feel they're already humble enough so they would not need to develop the trait of humility. And many might feel that humility, like integrity or character, cannot be taught or learned. You have it or you don't, so reading a book on it would not add to their "humility quotient."

Pope Francis would disagree with all of them.

He believes that authentic humility empowers leaders like no other leadership quality. "If we can develop a truly humble attitude, we can change the world," wrote Bergoglio before becoming pope. And he misses no opportunity to show that a person can never be too humble and that people can *learn* to be more humble. In doing so, he has altered the standards by which we measure our leaders.

✦ HUMILITY CHANGES EVERYTHING

Long before he was elected, Bergoglio set his sights on changing the culture of the Vatican, though he knew it would take years. In one of his best-known homilies, Pope Francis explains the problem: "In the prevailing culture, priority is given to the outward, the immediate, the visible, the quick, the superficial, and the provisional. What is real gives way to appearances." In other words, Francis believes that today's society places too much value on material things, the "visible" and "immediate" and "superficial." This is certainly not the world he envisions or desires.

Francis has said that humility and a life of material wealth are incompatible. "We have to be humble, but with real humility, from head-to-toe." To execute the cultural change he sought, Francis knew that he would have to set an unambiguous example as a pontiff who favored the real over the illusory, who valued substance over style, and who favored the poor over the rich.

A more humble pope emerged within minutes of his election at the conclave. One reporter described Bergoglio's elevation to pope one day after being elected: "His humility is already becoming legendary. Even when he was to be presented for the first time, he declined the use of a platform that would have elevated him above the other cardinals, instead preferring to remain at the same height as they. '*I'll stay down here,*' he is reported to have said. He then asked for a prayer for himself before administering a papal blessing to the crowd, yet another break from tradition."

In that simple gesture, he showed his humility, and not just for humility's sake. He wanted the world to know that he did not perceive his role as someone above the rest of humanity; Francis believes that no one is greater than any other human being, and that includes nonbelievers as well. A younger Bergoglio speaks of the importance of believing in the greatness of all people—and treating all with respect and dignity: "As I am a believer, I know that these riches are a gift from God. I also know that the other person, the atheist, does not know that. . . . I respect him and I show myself as I am. Where there is knowledge, there begins to appear esteem, affection, and friendship. . . . I am convinced that I do not have the right to make a judgment about the honesty of that person. . . . Everyone has a series of virtues, qualities and a greatness of his own."

Francis's earliest acts as pontiff offer several important leadership lessons. First, if you are fortunate enough to lead people, never use that position for selfish reasons. Take care not to do things that signal to your direct reports and other workers or colleagues that you are above them. That may mean moving out of the corner office to an inside office or even a cubicle. Many effective leaders have done exactly that.

According to *Forbes* magazine, a CEO who opts for a cubicle over a plush office sets a powerful example. That act says, "I am not above you; I am one of you, and I make mistakes, get angry, and live through the same things you do."

Forbes contributor Helen Coster, citing April Callis, president of a management consulting firm, explains the cubicle strategy, " 'If the CEO's goal is to make sure that everyone knows he's part of a team, sitting in a cubicle is an excellent way to demonstrate that. . . . You hear things that you wouldn't hear if you were ensconced in a corporate suite. Being in a cubicle gives you a strong dose of reality.' "

Former eBay CEO Meg Whitman occupied a small cubicle when she ran the company from the firm's San Jose base. The same was true of Michelle Peluso when she was the head of Travelocity. Zappos chief executive Tony Hsieh chose to work out of a cube in the firm's Las Vegas head office—and not just any cube, but one in which he was visible to all company visitors. At investment research firm Morningstar, all desks are placed side by side, and its CEO's desk is right alongside everyone else's in the investment services group. Even billionaire Michael Bloomberg, former mayor of New York City, used a cubicle when he was on the job.

There are other things leaders can do to demonstrate authentic humility. For example, they can lower their own salaries. There is a growing list of leaders who take $1 a year, since they usually make millions in stock options (especially if the company performs well). The $1-a-year salary helps to send an important message to employees: "If we all don't succeed, then I don't deserve a fat salary." Leaders who opted for the $1 salary include Larry Ellison of Oracle; Sergey Brin, Larry Page, and Eric Schmidt of Google; Elon Musk of Tesla; John Mackey of Whole Foods; and Mark Zuckerberg of Facebook. Others include N. R. Narayana Murthy, cofounder of Infosys; Pantas Sutardja and Sehat Sutardja of Marvell Technology Group; and Muhammad Ali Jinnah, who accepted only one rupee as the first governor-general of Pakistan (and also refused all other forms of compensation).

You can also demonstrate humility by spending company funds more wisely. If you tend to spend an inordinate amount of money for office or holiday parties, simplify them, scale them down, and let your employees suggest and vote on a good cause to which the extra money could be contributed.

Similarly, if you host a monthly leadership dinner at an expensive restaurant or fancy resort with other executives, curtail that practice and urge your leaders to host simpler, less expensive events such as monthly breakfasts with the folks closest to the customers. The two-way communication that results from those informal gatherings can yield great benefits that transcend but include the boosting of morale.

⊕ THE MOST HUMBLE FOCUS ON SERVICE

If Francis's focus on the least fortunate in society was not clear to everyone with his first acts and decisions, there was little ambiguity remaining after he delivered his first homily at the inaugural mass six days after becoming pope on March 19, 2013. Pope Francis proclaimed:

> *Let us never forget that authentic power is service, and that the Pope, too, when exercising power, must enter ever more fully into that service. . . . He must be inspired by the lowly, concrete, and faithful service which marked Saint Joseph and, like him, he must open his arms to protect all of God's people and embrace with tender affection the whole of humanity, especially the poorest, the weakest, the least important, those whom Matthew lists in the final judgment on love: the hungry, the thirsty, the stranger, the naked, the sick and those in prison. Only those who serve with love are able to protect!*

In his first month as pope, Francis expounded on the necessity of service and how that imperative included him as well. He said, "Christians are called to do the great work of evangelizing to the ends of the world in a spirit of humility rather than an attitude of conquering." He also asserted, "Preaching the gospel requires humility, service, charity, brotherly love. To approach evangelization with an imperialism or attitude of conquering doesn't work."

The pope as a *servant* to the people he leads almost seems like a contradiction, but not to Pope Francis, and it shouldn't to any effective leader, for that matter. For the pontiff, serving his people—serving *all* people—is expected and the way to become closer to the Highest

Being. Bergoglio wrote, "Jesus says that the one who rules must be like a servant. For me, that idea is valid for the religious person in any denomination. The true power of religious leadership comes from service."

If you change your view of your role as a leader—from one who gives orders to members of your team to one who *serves* your reports—you open up opportunities that did not exist before. This change doesn't have to be formal or regimented. In fact, Francis, similar to other great CEOs, has shown us that there is great power in informality.

To see the opportunities informality can create in action, ask each of your employees to share a cup of coffee in the company cafeteria or local coffee shop, either as a team, one at a time, or both (first meet with all, then one at a time; always go from macro to micro). Make it clear that you want to do everything within your power to help them achieve *their* goals. Also, make it known that you have a 24/7 open-door policy and that they are free to come see you at any time. Then just sip coffee and talk.

One former Fortune 100 CEO was known for keeping a huge bowl of candy and chocolates on his desk for his employees. They were told to come in as often as they wanted to grab as much candy as they wanted. That proved to be a very effective way to get people to stop by his office so he could simply ask, "How are things going?" That often led to far lengthier conversations that helped both the CEO and the employee to learn things neither knew before—and helped the leader engage the employee in a meaningful dialogue.

Engaging people in an in-depth conversation is near the top of Pope Francis's leadership to-do list. However, dialogue can happen only when both parties are open to it and respect the other. In 2010, Bergoglio said, "Dialogue is born from a respectful attitude toward the other person, from a conviction that the other person has something good to say. It supposes that we can make room in our heart for their point of view, their opinion, and their proposals. Dialogue entails a warm reception and not a preemptive condemnation. To dialogue, one must know how to lower the defenses, to open the doors of one's home and to offer warmth."

However, Bergoglio has always been a pragmatist and understood the roadblocks to successful communication. Here, he details all of the negativity that could interfere with meaningful conversations. When you read these words, make a mental note of how many of these barriers exist in your organization. "There are many barriers in everyday life that impede dialogue: misinformation, gossip, prejudices, defamation, and slander. All of these realities make up a certain cultural sensationalism that drowns out any possibility of openness to others. Thus, dialogue and encounter falter."

Here are a few ideas to help you get your feet firmly on that path to greater humility:

- *Don't Abuse Your Power As a Leader:* There can be no humility in leaders who place themselves above the people they are paid to serve. If you think that you might be taking advantage of your position, sit down with *your* boss or manager and ask for his or her opinion. Chances are your boss knows the truth. Like the $1-a-year CEOs, come up with your own ideas for showing the people who work for you that you are not only their boss but a colleague as well.

- *Eliminate Any Barriers That Set You Above Your Employees:* Look around your office. Is it inviting or intimidating? How far away is it from your employees? Is it closed off, while the rest of the office is open? How many gatekeepers would someone have to pass to get to it? Do you use the common kitchen and bathroom, or do you have private facilities? How many of the employees who are below your direct reports in the corporate hierarchy do you pass in the hallway each day? How many would you like to pass? Do you say hello to any of them? Remove the figurative papal thrones from your office. All of these things can be fixed to bring you closer to your people.

● *Refrain from Ultraexpensive Dinners That Only Top Management May Attend:* Instead, encourage all of your leaders to host a monthly breakfast with their direct employees. This will prove to be a much better use of your budgets and your time. If you are accustomed to hosting off-site meetings solely for senior managers, consider off-site meetings for middle managers and their direct reports as well.

CHAPTER 2

Smell Like Your Flock

One of the most oft-quoted Francisisms is his directive to "smell like your flock," which means immersing yourself deeply in whatever group you lead, or aspire to lead, and in a meaningful way. Like so many other things, this leadership principle has deep roots in his career. To understand its evolution, let's go back to the time Bergoglio became known as the "Bishop of the Slums."

✦ THE BISHOP OF THE SLUMS

When Bergoglio was "made an assistant bishop, back in the city of his birth," talented Francis biographer Paul Vallely explains, "an extraordinary journey had begun. It was to transform Jorge Mario Bergoglio into the Bishop of the Slums, a passionate defender of the disenfranchised, an unwavering enthusiast for dialogue as a way to build bridges between people of all backgrounds and beliefs."

According to those closest to Bergoglio, his years in the slums were decisive in making him a vocal defender of the least fortunate in society. One of Bergoglio's key priorities was to significantly increase the Church's involvement in the poorest, most dangerous parts of his jurisdiction. His war on drugs in the slums of Buenos Aires best illustrates how.

Paco—a cheap and dangerous form of cocaine—was the drug of choice for the poor in the slums, and it was everywhere. To combat this evil, several of Bergoglio's priests established programs to cure as many of the drug-addicted as possible. They established *Hogar de Cristo*, a rehab center, as well as two farms where addicts could work while they were kicking their *paco* habits.

Since nearly half of the inhabitants of those slums were under the age of 16, the priests launched a number of educational programs in order to give those young people a chance for complete rehabilitation. They included a scout group known as the "Explorers." Yet the most successful course of action was the apprenticeship program. That plan proved to be a way out of the slums, as the kids could apprentice to become anything from electricians to stonemasons or metalworkers. Suddenly, "*parroquia* (the parish) looked [like] an alternative to *paco*."

Bergoglio's mission in the slums was not without its hazards, however. One day, one of the most seasoned priests of the slums, Padre Pepe, was stopped in the streets and threatened by a stranger. He was told, in no uncertain terms, that if he did not stop his anti-drug activities, he would be finished.

Padre Pepe contacted Bergoglio immediately and told him of the threat he had received and of his fear for his own life. The two men met, and Bergoglio told him that if one of them had to die, he preferred it be himself. This statement, made without bravado, shows Bergoglio's commitment to his mission, and it speaks to the conviction leaders must have in their duties.

Author Vallely tells the dramatic story that played out next: "The day after Pepe was threatened, the archbishop [Bergoglio] held an outdoor Mass in the Plaza de Mayo, the city's main gathering point. . . . Television crews had been briefed that Archbishop Bergoglio [would be there]. When he reached the sermon Bergoglio delivered a bold denunciation of the drug traffickers and their death threats. He called them *los mercaderes de las tinieblas*, the merchants of darkness. In defiance he elevated Padre Pepe to a new position of the Vicar of All Slums. . . . Just like the Bible says, if a pastor is hurt, the flock will disperse. Bergoglio understood this and the fact that he said Mass spoke volumes."

After the threat and his public statement against it, Bergoglio spent much more time in the slums, meeting frequently with many members of the parish, blessing them, and eating biscuits and drinking *mate* (Argentina's favorite national tea). Bergoglio, through deeds more than words, made it clear that his priests were not to be harmed (and if they were, they would then have to tangle with a bishop who'd once worked as a bouncer). The "Bishop of the Slums" even volunteered to sleep in Padre Pepe's house in the slum to serve as an ever-present reminder that he was behind his mission absolutely.

Bergoglio became such a fixture of the slums that some members of the parish began to call him *El Chabon* ("The Dude"). He would walk down alleyways by himself, unafraid of the people who lived there. He even posed for pictures with anyone who asked. These were the people whom Bergoglio, pre-Francis, felt most at home with. He even washed the feet of some of the youngest who were hooked on *paco*. According to one of his aides, Bergoglio felt most comfortable with "those that had been tossed on life's 'existential garbage pile.' "

✢ SMELL YOUR FLOCK THE FRANCIS WAY

What can you do to immerse yourself in the institutions that you lead—or aspire to lead? In early 2014, we saw Francis-like leadership in action from a most unlikely place: the halls of the U.S. Congress.

I use the word "unlikely" because it is known in the United

States and around the world that the U.S. Congress is one of the least popular institutions in the entire country (with approval numbers down around 10 percent).

However, poor approval numbers did not stop Representative Steve Horsford, a Democrat from Nevada up for reelection in November 2014. This congressman felt that he was starting to lose touch with the people he was elected to represent. As a result, he decided that it was time for him to leave the suit and tie at home and take on a more typical job that someone in his district might hold.

So which company did he choose? He opted for United Parcel Service (UPS) and went to work clad all in brown, with short sleeves—the whole uniform. In his new, albeit brief, role, Horsford teamed up with another UPS employee, a driver, who helped the congressman to deliver packages in his Las Vegas district. "I'm Congressman Horsford. I'm here to deliver your package," he told one surprised package recipient.

It is important to note both the context and the zeitgeist that caused Representative Horsford to go "undercover" in his district. At the time, in early 2014, there were two debates related to wages and compensation raging in the United States and around the world.

Horsford's main object in this unconventional departure from his day job was to bring more attention to the national debate on minimum wage. At the time the congressman did his stint as a UPS package-delivery man, the minimum wage per hour in the United States was $7.25 per hour. However, there was a movement afoot to "give America a raise" to $10.10 per hour. Supporters of the minimum wage increase like Horsford argued that most families who rely on a minimum wage job have a hard time putting food on the table without help from the U.S. government.

Horsford's actions echo one of Pope Francis's top priorities, which is shining the light on the problem of extreme income inequality. Remember the incredible statistic that was discussed in the Prologue: The eighty-five wealthiest people in the world control more wealth than half of the world—that is, more wealth than 3.5 billion of the poorest people on the planet. The issue of minimum wage (and low wages in general) is not just an American challenge—it is a global one. And few people understand this better than Pope Francis. He knows that the low wages in many countries exacerbate the income equality debacle.

In retrospect, Horsford could have selected a more suitable company than UPS for his experiment. Why? UPS is one of the better employers in terms of compensation. Entry-level positions at UPS pay $12 per hour, which is almost $2 more than the target minimum of $10.10 per hour. Drivers at UPS earn $32.50 per hour.

So while the congressman wanted to highlight UPS as a shining example of a company that pays its workers fairly, he could have made a far more meaningful statement by working for an employer that actually paid the minimum wage, like McDonald's or another fast-food or retail company. It is important to smell like your flock—but it makes a big difference which members of the flock you "smell" like.

✥ TAKING A PAGE FROM ENGLAND'S "WALMART"

The next "flock" example involves Tesco PLC, which has operations in twelve countries, spanning Europe, Asia, and North America, and is the United Kingdom's largest seller of groceries. By profits, the U.K. retailer is the second largest in the world, and the third largest if measured by revenues (France's Carrefour is second).

For a long time, however, Tesco was considered a second-tier company. It actually lost 1 to 2 percent of revenues per year during each year of the 1990s.

How did Tesco's managers turn things around? They decided to smell like their flock.

Tesco has a unique program that requires all its front-office executives and the managers in departments such as distribution to work more traditional store jobs for a full week every year. The program is dubbed TWIST, for "Tesco Week in Store Together." From Tesco: "TWIST reinforces our values and aims to improve knowledge-sharing throughout the company . . . . It covers all aspects of store operations, from the back door to the shop floor working as a Customer Assistant, including: receiving deliveries, working in the warehouse, filling, working on checkouts and the Customer Service Desk and this year completing a nightshift."

TWIST is only a part of what helped Tesco grow to become the largest retailer in Europe. However, this is the type of program that brings people at the top of an organization closer to those who get the real work done and, more important, closer to customers. That is certainly a Pope Francis–like leadership imperative.

Here is how Michael Trimmer of *Christian Today* viewed Francis about six months after he had become pope: "It's difficult to completely evade the pomp and ceremony of leading the world's single largest religious denomination, but since the Pope is the first to hail from the Jesuit order, he very firmly believes in the importance of being a man of his people. After all, how can he share in their passions and pain if he is not a part of their world in some small way?"

A program like TWIST is a great idea for getting leaders higher up in the hierarchy to "share in the passions and pain" of the people who make up the greatest numbers in the organization. Put another way, it forces managers to get out of their plush, corner offices and into the stores, where the real heartbeat of the company lies.

What additional steps can you take to more effectively smell like your flock? Here are a few more ideas:

- *Manage by Walking Around:* Manage by Walking Around (MBWA) became popular years ago but is making a comeback today. This technique was how Bill Hewlett and David Packard managed their computer company. Steve Jobs, of Apple fame, also lived by this management principle and included customers in the mix as well by calling them in order to get their assessments of the latest Apple product.

  Before providing additional tips on MBWA, let's see if you are a natural or need a little help. Please ask yourself these questions:

  1. Do you feel like you have your pulse on the inner workings of your department?

  2. Do you feel that you know the strengths, weaknesses, and current morale of each of your direct reports?

  3. Do you regularly have unscheduled, informal discussions with your people?

  If you answered no to at least one of these questions, try these tips from Anne Fisher of Fortune.com—mixed in with a few extra ideas: Make MBWA a regular and frequent thing. Consider using different restrooms so you can conveniently bump into new people all the time. Never bring an aide or an entourage, and over time make sure you get to everybody in all departments. Ask each person for one great idea on how to make things better, and recognize the ones you implement. Do not criticize; asking for suggestions is more of a fact-finding mission, so learn to hold your tongue.

⬭ *If Your Organization Cannot Implement a Full TWIST-like Program, Try These Alternative Ideas:* If you can, urge your leaders to spend at least a day doing someone else's job. It is still an effective method that gives leaders an opportunity to better understand the needs and issues of colleagues further down the organization's food chain.

⬭ *To Better Understand Your Own "Flock," Get Them out of the Office and into Social Settings:* I know one former Fortune 500 CEO who hosted barbeques for his employees at least once a year. If that doesn't work for you, come up with other ideas for getting your direct reports out of the office into a social setting. For example, give them an extra hour or two off by taking them out for a monthly happy hour in order to get them into a more informal setting.

CHAPTER 3

Who Am I to Judge?

To Pope Francis, words matter. He puts great care into each word and sentence in his books and homilies. He says, or does, very little by accident. This is one of the reasons so many Catholics search everything he writes for clues as to where he intends to take the Catholic Church.

✦ "WHO AM I TO JUDGE?"

In late July 2013, Pope Francis held a press conference on a return flight from Buenos Aires. A reporter had asked Francis about the "gay lobby," which, six weeks earlier, he said did exist inside the Vatican. After making a joke, the pope grew more thoughtful and said that it was important to distinguish between individuals and more detrimental lobbies. "[A] lobby of the greedy, a lobby of politicians, a lobby of the masons, so many lobbies." He then delivered the line that NBC News would call his most important phrase of the year. "A gay person who is seeking God, who is of good will—well, who am I to judge him?" NBC News asked, "Could five little words change the course of the Catholic Church?"

Let's delve deeper to see where that sentiment originated. In August 2013, the pope granted an interview to the editor in chief of

La Civiltà Cattolica, the Italian Jesuit journal, in which he explained why he felt that it was not his place to judge people who might be different from others, especially those who might be shunned by society for reasons beyond their control. Here is how Archbishop Bergoglio said he dealt with this difficult social issue back home before taking on the papacy: "In Buenos Aires I used to receive letters from homosexual persons who are 'socially wounded' because they tell me that they feel like the church has always condemned them. But the church does not want to do this. During the return flight from Rio de Janeiro I said that if a homosexual person is of good will and in search of God, *I am no one to judge.*"

✦ Don't Judge—Assess

Pope Francis is telling us in this statement that there is a substantial distinction between "judging" and "assessing" people. Only a power higher than a pope can judge a person. And judgments should never be made as a consequence of a person's color, creed, illness, station in life, sexual orientation, or anything else he or she may not control.

However, assessing, which is more akin to decision making, is done by leaders all the time. For example, Francis made a severe assessment of the "bling bishop" mentioned in the Prologue, deciding he was not the sort of leader who fit his vision of a Church focused on assisting the poorest and least fortunate in society. And yet Francis did not personally criticize him; his assessment was that Bishop Franz-Peter Tebartz-van Elst's choices were simply not the right fit for Francis's view of the Catholic Church.

If you lead, or aspire to lead, people in an organization, then you must make many assessments every day. Think of the job you have right now. Before deciding to join your organization, you had to assess the company or organization—the location, pay package, and opportunity for advancement. However, it is unlikely that any of the assessments that you made—or continue to make—are more important than the assessments you make of *people*. That is the Pope Francis imperative: people first, and then everything else follows.

If you lead people, you must assess a great number of constituencies, from bosses to suppliers, and then to customers. The most important assessments, however, are those you make of your direct reports. They count on you for an honest and direct assessment on a regular basis, and they deserve no less. We are all familiar with performance reviews, but the most effective leaders do not wait for that once-a-year ritual; instead, they make a habit of assessing people and discussing that assessment with the individual on a regular basis, in both formal and informal situations. And it is important, says Francis, not to deliver a monologue when speaking with your people and to take into account the changing nature of our culture. "Dialog must be serious, without fear, [and] sincere," Francis told interviewer Antonio Spadaro. "It is important to recall that the language of young people in formation today is different from that in the past," said Francis. He added, "Those who work with youth cannot be content with simply saying things that are too tidy and structured, as in a tract; these things go in one ear and out the other of young people. We need a new language, a new way of saying things."

In his most prominent homily, Francis discusses the importance of listening to your people. "Today more than ever we need men and women who, on the basis of their experience of accompanying others, are familiar with the processes which call for prudence, understanding, patience. . . . We need to practice the art of listening, which is more than simply hearing. Listening, in communication, is an openness of heart, which makes possible that closeness without genuine spiritual encounter cannot occur. Listening helps us to find the right gesture and word, which shows that we are more than simple bystanders. Only through such respectful and compassionate listening can we enter on the paths of true growth."

Pope Francis learned early in his career to make sure that he trusted people completely unless, and until, they proved themselves to be unreliable. He learned to always give people the benefit of the doubt. "When I entrust something to someone, I totally trust that person. He or she must make a really big mistake before I rebuke that person."

Francis goes to great lengths to put people on an equal and even footing when engaging others in conversation. For example, pope watchers took note when Francis met with the Latin American and Caribbean Confederation of Religious Men and Women in the summer of 2013. Did he sit above these people, as was the case with so many pontiffs before him? According to two prominent reporters, Massimo Franco and Michael Sean Winters, he did not: "He [Pope Francis] sat with them in a circle, on a chair the same kind as theirs; 'they were having a conversation,'" as Winters, the reporter for *The National Catholic Reporter* explained.

Franco continued, "There is a striking difference between the photographs of this meeting and the images of US bishops on their *ad limina* visit the year before, he added. 'In those photos, the pope sat on his throne, the bishops sat in chairs in single file . . . lined up like altar boys. The pope read from his prepared remarks. They listened. No conversation.'"

Others have remarked that Pope Francis works hard to make people feel comfortable and on equal footing rather than beneath him. Francis the pope is also not above assessment from Francis the man. In an interview with an Italian journalist, the pope considered the mistakes he made much earlier in his career. "My authoritarian and quick manner of making decisions led me to have serious problems and to be accused of being ultraconservative. I have never been a right-winger. . . . It was my authoritarian way of making decisions that created problems."

In addition, the pope believes that the most important assessments involve consultation with others, but he admitted that in the past he fell short in that category as well. "I did not always do the necessary consultation. And this was not a good thing. My style of government as a Jesuit at the beginning had many faults. That was a difficult time for society. . . . Because of this, I found myself provincial when I was still very young. I was only 36 years old. That was crazy. I had to deal with difficult situations, and I made my decisions abruptly and by myself."

But there is much evidence that he's sharpened his game. In 2013, Francis selected eight cardinals representing five continents to serve as an advisory panel on global issues. To Vatican watchers, this unprecedented assembly of a consulting group was a real game-changer. If Pope Francis was CEO Francis, he would now have his carefully selected board of directors firmly in place. To guard against insularity, the pope made sure only one cardinal came from Italy. According to political columnist Massimo Franco, assembling such a group marked a potentially important turning point for the Vatican: "It was a novel move that fed rumors of a new style of governance, and even a collegial future in which power would be shared at the very top of the Holy See."

✦ WHAT TO ASSESS

Now that we have established the importance of honest and frequent assessments of your people, we should focus on precisely *what* you should be assessing. Many leaders focus on improving their people's weaknesses to make them better at their jobs. That is the wrong way to proceed. We now have a huge body of research showing that the best way to become an expert in any field comes through accumulating years of specific, hands-on experience in one particular field—at least ten thousand hours, a study popularized by Malcolm Gladwell in his bestselling book, *Outliers*. Gladwell tells us of such diverse people and groups as Bill Gates of Microsoft fame, football receiving great Jerry Rice, and the Beatles. What do all three have in common? Each put in a very grueling ten thousand hours of very specific practice in their field. The way to enhance people's performance, other than giving them the time to live up to Gladwell's ten-thousand-hour ideal, is to focus on enhancing their strengths.

Pope Francis naturally sees the best in people and ignores their shortcomings, particularly if that person has suffered or experienced a hardship. He also discourages us from becoming negative or giving in to defeatism. "One of the most serious temptations which stifles boldness and zeal is a defeatism which turns us into querulous and disillusioned pessimists, 'sourpusses.' If we start without confidence, we have already lost half the battle and we bury our talents. While painfully aware of our own frailties, we have to march on without giving in."

Pope Francis's emphasis on confidence and eschewing negativity comports itself nicely with the burgeoning body of knowledge on strengths-based leadership. For instance, John H. Zenger and Joseph Folkman, in *The Extraordinary Leader*, identify "[t]he sixteen behaviors (competencies) that make a difference in how leaders are perceived by others." The sixteen traits include such things as "focusing on results," "establishing stretch goals," "inspiring and motivating others to high performance," and "championing change."

The key to Zenger and Folkman's extensive research—based on data gathered from twenty thousand leaders—is that it is far more important to focus on strengths than on weaknesses. Managers with no perceived strengths were rated in the bottom third of all leaders. However, the ranking of a manager with at least one perceived strength went from the bottom third all the way to the sixty-eighth percentile. The rating of a manager who was perceived to have three of the sixteen strengths rose all the way to the eighty-fourth percentile. In other words, concluded Zenger, it is far better to focus on just a few strengths rather than all sixteen, and better to leave a person's weaknesses out of the equation altogether.

This is absolutely critical to keep in mind when it comes to assessing people. Instead of nitpicking or looking for mediocrity, focus on enhancing their strengths. Pope Francis is not an academic, but he still understands the importance of lifting people up. "We have to regard ourselves as sealed, even branded, by this mission of bringing light, blessing, enlivening, raising up, healing, and feeling. All around us we begin to see nurses with soul, teachers with soul, politicians with soul, people who have chosen deep down to be with others and for others."

What can you do to make better assessments and ensure that you are not judging your people? Here are a few ideas:

- *Always Remember Pope Francis's Five Words "Who Am I to Judge?":* As a leader, you must be sure to leave at the door any biases that you may have against anyone or any group under your leadership. Just as important, even if you are a skeptical type, you must learn to trust your people unless they give you a reason not to.

- *True Dialogue Is a Two-Way Conversation:* When engaging in dialogue with your people, remember that listening is just as important—if not more important—than talking. Spend all your time talking, and you will do nothing but confirm your own biases and prejudices. Spend your time listening, and you will gain new perspectives and learn your reports' goals, desires, and strengths. If you involve your team in true dialogue, you will be able to help them improve their work, which will ultimately make you a better manager.

- *Focus on Strengths:* With each of your direct reports, start with a clean piece of paper. Make a list of their strengths to ensure that all of your people are in the right jobs. Do not assume just because someone has been in a job for years that he or she belongs there. Empower your employees to develop their strengths as well. If they want to take a class that conflicts with their work schedule, give them flexible hours if possible. Allow them to take opportunities within your organization as well, if the opportunities are aligned with their strengths.

CHAPTER 4

Don't Change—Reinvent

C asual Francis watchers might think that the pope wakes up every so often with an incredible idea backed up by an equally stunning proclamation. For example, in the first week of March 2014, just days shy of his one-year anniversary as pontiff, Francis did not evade a single question about same-sex civil unions. In an interview with Ferruccio de Bortoli of the Italian daily *Corriere della Sera*, Francis said that states seek "to regularize different situations of living together" in order to ensure healthcare and other economic benefits. And he also said, "We have to look at the different cases and evaluate them in their variety." Opening the door to possible same-sex unions in the Catholic Church was unthinkable before Francis.

About two weeks before that interview, Pope Francis discussed the topic of divorce. It is common knowledge that divorce has never been sanctioned by the Catholic Church. However, just because something is not acceptable to the Church does not prohibit Pope Francis from doing his job of serving his people.

Vatican Radio summed up Pope Francis's fresh approach to the issue of divorce. "Pope Francis celebrated Mass . . . this morning. In remarks following the readings . . . the Holy Father focused on the beauty of marriage and warned that the Church must accompany—not condemn—those who experience failure in married life. He explained that Christ is the Bridegroom of the Church, and therefore you cannot understand one without the other."

About two months later, in late April 2014, Pope Francis did something that surprised the world while underscoring his continued attention to the issue of divorce and communion. In September 2013, Pope Francis had received a letter from a woman named Jacqueline Sabetta Lisbona, who asked whether she could receive the sacrament of communion even though her husband had been previously divorced. According to the woman's husband, Pope Francis called his wife in response to the letter to discuss the issue of communion in relation to Vatican law. Ms. Lisbona, from the pope's home country of Argentina, was reportedly told by Francis that she could participate in the sacrament of communion, despite the fact that her husband had been divorced and remarried. If true, this would mark a huge change in Vatican tradition. For the record, it was Ms. Lisbona's husband who conveyed the contents of that potentially explosive phone call (and gave television interviews detailing the conversation). While Vatican officials acknowledged that the phone call took place, they would not discuss or reveal what had been said by Francis or Ms. Lisbona. Once again, we see the stealthy, clever ways in which Francis introduces a new and inclusive measure without necessarily discussing a definitive change in Catholic doctrine.

Prior to this, in February 2014, Francis had hosted a two-day meeting with the world's cardinals to discuss the changing stance of the Church on today's far more complex family situations such as divorce, contraception, and gay marriage. The 266th pontiff told the cardinals in attendance that Catholicism needs to be a far more accepting body that should take a "pastoral" approach that is "intelligent, courageous and full of love," instead of being fixated on some kind of the abstract or dated ideology.

These potential sea changes regarding civil unions and divorce were monumental. For thousands of years anyone who was divorced had been barred from participating in the most holy part of Catholic mass, Holy Communion (though this is not strictly enforced everywhere). And even though Pope Francis was not pronouncing any official Vatican-based change in doctrine as far as same-sex marriage is concerned, he at least left the door open to discussions about same-sex civil unions.

However, to the really close Francis watchers, these potential explosive changes should not have come as a big surprise. Ever since Francis answered "Who am I to judge?" when asked about gay marriage, it should have been apparent that this pope, as humble as he is, still has some very grand ambitions when it comes to reinventing the Catholic Church.

Whether his peers realized the extent of those ambitions when he was elected pope is not known, though he clearly wasn't the initial favorite at the cardinals' 2013 conclave. I believe, however, that the cardinals were seeking authentic change when they chose Bergoglio.

✤ BERGOGLIO'S CHOICE: THE 2005 CONCLAVE

Let's first turn the clock back to 2005 to better understand Bergoglio's ambitions. His actions tell us that he prefers to fly under the radar. Despite his accomplishments, to some close to him he did not seem like someone ambitious enough to become the head of one of the largest institutions in the world. But even those closest to Bergoglio couldn't really tell what he was thinking either way; he had grown too humble to wear any ambitions on his sleeve.

Regardless of his intentions, the conclave of 2005, in which Joseph Ratzinger was elected to the papacy, reveals quite a bit about the character of Jorge Mario Bergoglio. Going into that conclave, there were four possible choices that the 115 electors focused upon, and Bergoglio and Ratzinger were among those four. However, Bergoglio had a handicap. During the military overthrow of the Argentinean government in 1976, Bergoglio was accused of being involved in the kidnapping of two Jesuit priests. After dismissing the two priests for disobeying orders, they were kidnapped by the death squads and tortured. Bergoglio petitioned for their release, but even today he regrets not having done enough. Perhaps this is one of the acts that has led Pope Francis to label himself a "sinner" who consistently seeks God's forgiveness. In any event, this scandal led to a "Stop Bergoglio" file being circulated during the 2005 conclave. The surviving priest, Father Francisco Jalics, denied after the conclave that Bergoglio was to blame, though there are doubters who believe that Bergoglio informed the military of the priests' activities.

Despite that roadblock, Bergoglio came in second in each of the first three ballots, according to Francis biographer Paul Vallely. On the second ballot, while Ratzinger had chalked up 65 votes of a total of 115 possible votes, Bergoglio's support had increased by 300 percent, to 35 votes.

On the third ballot, Bergoglio received 40 votes, the most ever for a Latin American, and enough to block Ratzinger if he decided to do so. After that third ballot, however, Bergoglio thought through the possible outcomes. He knew that conclave rules hold that the two-thirds majority rule would give way to a simple majority after a certain length of time, so Ratzinger supporters could simply wait until only a majority of the votes would be needed. Bergoglio decided not to risk the reputation of the Church for his own personal ambition. He feared that a drawn-out vote with no winner for days would bring about an appearance of fighting factions and disharmony within the conclave.

Bergoglio began to quietly canvass not for himself, but for

Ratzinger. In other words, the only person Bergoglio campaigned for at the 2005 conclave was Cardinal Ratzinger. Not a single cardinal reported any self-promotion on the part of Bergoglio. If he wanted to be pontiff, he didn't tell any of his friends or peers. Perhaps he figured that the Church was not ready for the transformation he felt it needed. Or perhaps he felt unworthy of the Holy See (he called himself "a sinner who God in his mercy has chosen to love").

There is one more important point that has received little or no attention regarding the 2005 conclave. Bergoglio was almost seventy years old in 2005. He had no way of knowing that Ratzinger would ultimately resign. Thus, Bergoglio likely assumed that this would be his last chance to become pope. Yet he still put the image of the Church above his own personal goals. That act of humble generosity provides more insight into the selflessness and authenticity of the man who would be pope eight years later.

✤ SELECTING AN EXPLOSIVE REFORMER: THE 2013 CONCLAVE

After Benedict XVI's nearly unprecedented act of stepping down as the 265th pope, it was clear that there was a division among the cardinals when it came to choosing the next pope. One group wanted the ways of the Curia and the principles of the Catholic Church safeguarded, preferring someone who would not rock the proverbial boat. However, another group felt strongly that the Church needed an unbowed reformer, someone who would help people forget the scandal-ridden eight-year tenure of Pope Benedict XVI, someone who would not only change the outdated traditions of yesterday but also, and more important, forge a new and more relevant path forward for the Catholic Church.

"In the final days, as Congregations gave way to conclave, the discussions moved," Cardinal Cormac Murphy-O'Connor told Pope Francis's biographer Paul Vallely, "from just the need for good governance to the need for a Pope deeply rooted in the gospel—a new style in the Church and a new style of papacy."

The cardinals had no clear front-runner, but the media did: Cardinal Angelo Scola of Milan. One local newspaper, *Corriere della Sera*, boldly announced that Cardinal Scola already had 50 votes going into the conclave, only 22 votes shy of gaining the papacy!

During the conclave, each cardinal is allowed five minutes to make a speech to the others. Yet Cardinal Scola's speech inspired little enthusiasm, failing to impress the other cardinals. The brief, three-and-a-half minute speech that the cardinals took note of, however, the one speech that became the talk of the conclave, was of course Jorge Mario Bergoglio's oration, spoken in Italian.

He said, "The only purpose of the Church is to go out and tell the world the good news about Jesus Christ. It needed to surge forth to the peripheries, not just geographically but to the existential peripheries where people grappled with sin, pain, injustice, ignorance, and indifference to religion."

He continued, "But the Church got too wrapped up in itself. . . . It had become 'self-referential,' which had made it sick. It was suffering a 'kind of theological narcissism.' . . . A self-referential Church wants to keep Jesus to itself, instead of letting him out to others. . . . Put simply, there are two images of [the] Church; a church which evangelizes and comes out of herself or a worldly church, living within itself, of herself, for herself. The next Pope should be someone who helps the Church surge forth to the peripheries like a sweet and comforting mother who offers the joy of Jesus to the world."

That short speech was not only well received, it captivated the hearts and minds of the other cardinals. One person exhilarated by the Bergoglio speech was Cardinal Christoph Schönborn, who said in low tones to the cardinal next to him, *"That's what we need"* [italics mine].

Cardinal Murphy-O'Connor agreed with Cardinal Schönborn. "Bergoglio was the first man not to be introspective about the problems of the Church, but to be outgoing—He was more spiritual and more theological—and, as several cardinals said in the same shared phrase afterwards, 'he spoke from the heart.' It was very simple, very spiritual, and it touched on the urgent necessity for renewal."

✦ REFORM, RENEWAL, AND REINVENTION

We now know that Bergoglio's speech was a sign of things to come. It was subtle but also authoritative. It was vintage Bergoglio—speaking the truth—while maintaining his humility.

It would require five ballots for Bergoglio to be elected at that 2013 conclave. As the cardinals voted for the fifth and final time, insiders said that Bergoglio's demeanor was one of seriousness, but he also appeared somewhat stunned. It was as if he knew what was about to happen and he felt the weight of the world on his shoulders.

As the votes were tallied, and it was revealed that Cardinal Jorge Mario Bergoglio had exceeded the necessary 77 votes required (he received 90), the other cardinals broke out in applause in the otherwise quiet Sistine Chapel. There was a new pope, one with scores of ideas to reinvent the Catholic Church.

Finally, it was time for Bergoglio to officially accept the office of the papacy to which he had just been elected. The assistant dean of cardinals then put this question to Jorge Mario Bergoglio: *"Acceptasne electionem de te canonice factam in Summum Pontificem?"* he inquired. ("Do you accept your canonical election as Supreme Pontiff?")

"*Accepto*" has been the traditional response for centuries.

However, Bergoglio said, "I am a great sinner, trusting in the mercy and patience of God in suffering, I accept."

Even at this moment, at the pinnacle of his life and career, Bergoglio could not simply set aside his sins. His humility would not permit it. Francis's biographer explained what happened next.

The assistant cardinal put one final question to Bergoglio: "*Quo nomine vis vocari?*" ("What name do you take?")

"*Vocabor Franciscus.*" ("I will be called Francis.")

"At the name the cardinals cheered. But no pope had ever taken the name Francis before. Some eyebrows were raised. More than a few wondered what they had let themselves in for."

Massimo Franco, writer for *Corriere della Sera*, later summed up the new reformer pontiff: "Francis I, the first Jesuit Pope, represents a potential revolution. He was chosen as a reformer of the Curia, scandal-solver and director of a true globalization of the Vatican."

❖ Reinvent Your Organization

If your organization is in need of Franciscan reinvention, what steps can you take to turn things around? Always start with people and structure. Do you have the right people, and are they placed in the right positions? Does the structure of your organization maximize productivity, or are there places for improvement?

If you are a leader who hires other leaders, consider hiring an outsider—someone not mired in the years and mistakes of your organization's past, who has no allegiances to silos or office politics. Francis was the first Jesuit pope, the first South American pope, and at his election was considered an outsider to the ways of the Vatican.

Here are some other ideas you can implement to transform your organization:

- *Keep Your Organization Relevant:* Whether you manufacture goods or provide services, your company must have relevance in today's world. While later chapters go into greater detail about keeping your company relevant, remember Francis's spirit of reinvention upon his election; just because your company has done something one way for years doesn't mean it still works today.

- *Maintain the Greater Good:* Bergoglio selflessly took himself out of the 2005 running for the papacy by campaigning for Ratzinger, because he felt that a drawn-out election would reflect negatively on the greater Catholic Church. For your organization to be at its strongest, you need people willing to do what is for the greater good and not only look out for themselves. You can identify the self-interested people in your organization, because they often cling to the silos or cliques they have created in order to insulate themselves from organizational change. Though these people might get their jobs done, they are a detriment to overall culture. Fire anyone in your organization who does not live the values you have established. This recommendation has its roots in the corporate world, where some of the most effective leaders of the past three decades have implemented this imperative when they felt strongly about someone.

- *Make Your Office Efficient:* In most companies and other organizations, people do things a certain way only because they have done them that way for years. It might be time for you to spearhead a reinvention of your firm's processes. For example, say that you have a purchasing document that requires five signatures before it can be sent to a supplier; that could be a sign of a bloated bureaucracy. Ask yourself and your team why those five signatures are necessary, and reanalyze the original rationale for the process to find out if it is still valid. Streamline it by requiring the lowest possible number of approvals. Similarly, look at all of your processes to make sure that red tape is not killing your organization. You may also consider moving to a paperless office to eliminate even more needless bureaucracy.

CHAPTER 5

Make Inclusion a Top Priority

From his very first days as pope, Francis's top priority has been to make the Church more inclusive. This goal is something he has hoped for ever since his days as the "Bishop of the Slums." Those who know him best have said that he changed during those years when he strolled back alleys drinking *mata* with the poor and tending to his flock. He became closest with those who were otherwise alienated not only by society at large but by the ever-increasing opulence of the Catholic Church's high offices.

The quest for inclusion has been one of the most important factors in making Pope Francis so popular. Inclusion was at the heart of the majority of his key decisions during his first year as head of the Church. While he dismisses the depiction of himself as a "superhero" pontiff, there is no arguing how he has affected the 1.2 billion Catholics he leads (not to mention millions of others who have come to admire him). He may be no superhero, but he is the only pope in history to canonize two popes in a single day—Pope John XXIII and Pope John Paul II—in late April 2014. Papal pundits lauded the act because the two popes were seen as a "balance"—representing both the left and the right of the Church. But, overall, the tens of millions who watched the brief ceremony on their televisions were thrilled, not to mention the several hundreds of thousand who turned up at

St. Peter's Square in Rome to watch it all in person. After the canonization was complete, Francis mounted his popemobile so he could see and touch the huge throngs who had assembled for that historic ceremony.

However, that was a single act. It does not explain how Pope Francis motivated millions to return to the Church; it is *how* he has done it that is most pertinent to any discussion about inclusiveness.

✦ LEAVE NO ONE BEHIND

Some Francis watchers may think that there is an arbitrary or random order to his pronouncements. One week he is talking about not judging gay church members; the next he is talking about softening the Church's stance on divorce. While that is a possibility, I assert that Francis works in a far more systematic and methodical manner. Either way, he has demonstrated great skill at simultaneously leading and reforming while navigating his way through one of the largest, most insular and entrenched organizations in the world.

Francis has been able to execute deftly on his agenda of reinvention. He makes change with the full knowledge that there are powerful factions within the Church that think he has gone too far—and too fast—on social issues, such as the ones we have discussed in this and earlier chapters (e.g., civil unions and divorce).

Six months after he became pope, Francis said very directly that he does not see the Church as only for the purest among us; he sees the Church as a "home for all." He declared that the Church should not be a "small chapel focused on doctrine, orthodoxy and a limited agenda of moral teachings." His goal is a lofty one: Leave no one behind.

✦ "THE FIRST REFORM MUST BE THE ATTITUDE"

In the summer of 2013, Pope Francis granted an interview to Antonio Spadaro, a local journalist who regularly writes for Jesuit and other Catholic journals. In this illuminating interview, Francis explains that "the first reform must be the attitude."

He elaborates: "The ministers of the Gospel must be people who can warm the hearts of the people, who walk through the dark night with them, who know how to dialogue and to descend themselves into their people's night, into the darkness, but without getting lost. The people of God want pastors, not clergy acting like bureaucrats or government officials. The bishops, particularly, must be able to support the movements of God among their people with patience, so that no one is left behind. But they must also be able to accompany the flock that has a flair for finding new paths."

Let's unpack this important sentiment to reflect on Francis's intentions. First, he says how important it is that leaders of the Church attend to the neediest in our society, especially when they get lost, or are mired in poverty, or have fallen on difficult times. The Catholic clergy must be there for their congregation, no matter how bad their situation, and help bear their burdens (i.e., "walk through the dark night with them").

Francis then raises another one of his key themes—dialogue (i.e., "who know how to dialogue and to descend themselves into their people's night"). Francis has discussed the importance of dialogue often in his writings, homilies, and other works. He feels that few things are more important than having members of the clergy learn how to meaningfully engage with various constituencies, especially the youngest in society. Even before he became pope, he said, "Dialogue entails a warm reception and not a preemptive condemnation.

To dialogue, one must know how to lower the defenses, to open the doors of one's home and to offer warmth."

He contends, however, that there are many factors that interfere with effective communication between pastor and members of their flocks: "There are many barriers in everyday life that impede dialogue: misinformation, gossip, prejudices, defamation, and slander. All of these realities make up a certain cultural sensationalism that drowns out any possibility of openness to others. Thus, dialogue and encounter falter." The emphasis on dialogue again ties back to inclusion. The underserved Catholic population cannot be reached unless the clergy can empathetically communicate with them. Francis understands this from firsthand experience.

Next, he discusses just what it is that people need—and what they don't need—from the stewards of their church (i.e., "The people of God want pastors, not clergy acting like bureaucrats or government officials"). Here, he is serving notice to members of the clergy: It's people first, then paperwork. This is a simplistic way of saying that regardless of your level in the Church hierarchy, there is always more that you can do to help and comfort people in need than simply being just another administrator or paper-pusher.

The following Francis story hammers home the "people first" point. Soon after becoming pope, Francis explained to one of his archbishops what he expected of him. "You will not stay behind a desk signing parchments," the Holy Father told the archbishop. "Now I want you always among the people. In Buenos Aires, I often went out in the evening to go find the poor. Now I no longer can. It is difficult for me to leave the Vatican. You will do it for me." This brief story must be unprecedented in the Vatican. A relatively new pope tells an archbishop that his *top priority* is going into the night to reach out to poor people and help to get them fed, sheltered, and back on their feet. Whereas many would see the archbishop's job to manage the clergy beneath him, Pope Francis wants his highest-ranking clergy to have the most direct and impactful contact with their flock.

In one interview, Francis spoke directly to the topic of inclusion (i.e., "The bishops, particularly, must be able to support the movements of God among their people with patience, so that no one is left behind"). "Leaving no one behind" is, of course, the essence of Francis. Many people in different parts of society, such as in politics, talk about leaving no one behind (the example that most readily jumps to mind is George W. Bush's notorious No Child Left Behind education program), but few mean it. That is the difference between Pope Francis and so many other leaders in our society. Leaders in government and business often say something because they know that it is what various constituencies want to hear. But when Francis says something, he speaks from the truth of personal experience, and he operates not by appealing to influential minorities but by empowering the people he serves.

✦ PURSUE OUTSIDERS

In that same August interview with journalist Antonio Spadaro, the pontiff explains why it is so important to pursue and help everyone—not just those who have lived under strict Church doctrine. "Instead of being just a church that welcomes and receives by keeping the doors open, let us try also to be a church that finds new roads, that is able to step outside itself and go to those who do not attend Mass, to those who have quit or are different. The ones who quit sometimes do it for reasons that, if properly understood and assessed, can lead to a return. But that takes audacity and courage." Once again, Francis articulates his priorities while urging other members of the Church to follow his example. In the aforementioned quote, it is apparent that Francis wants members of the clergy to go the extra mile in helping people in any way they can, especially in bringing them back into the church.

"I can see clearly that the thing the church needs most today is the ability to heal wounds and to warm the hearts of the faithful; it needs nearness, proximity," explained Francis.

Wounded is another term that Francis has used liberally. He feels that the poor, downtrodden, and disenfranchised are like "the walking wounded," although it is their souls as well as their physical selves in dire need of attention. And that is where the pastor comes in. To be truly inclusive, the pastor needs to attend to the needs of the least fortunate and go to wherever these people reside.

✦ INCLUDE OTHERS IN DECISION MAKING

In addition to making the Church more inclusive, Francis made an unprecedented move by including others in his own decision-making process. As mentioned in Chapter 3, Francis pulled together a group of eight cardinals to counsel him on global issues. He made sure not to include only those cardinals who would tell him what he wanted to hear. The last thing Bergoglio or Francis wanted was a bunch of yes-men. Instead, he chose a wide variety of cardinals from different nations. Seven of the "gang of eight" or "Vatican 8" (V-8) cardinals Francis selected were from outside of Italy.

Many saw Francis's creation of an international advisory board as a bold move, but it also had its fair share of skeptics. According to Italian journalist Massimo Franco, "It was a novel move that fed rumors of a new style of governance, and even a collegial future in which power would be shared at the very top of the Holy See. That remains to be seen. As Father Federico Lombardi, the Vatican's spokesman, has repeatedly pointed out, '[I]t is the pope who decides. The eight cardinals just advise him.' "

This lesson of including and consulting with others has many applications to the world of business and society. The best leaders I have studied over the years always had people in their inner circle who would prove to be sounding boards on a whole host of issues.

Colin Powell, U.S. Army general and former secretary of state, has explained just how lonely it is at the top of any organization. This is why it is so important to surround yourself with people who are not afraid to tell you the truth and, as important, who have the capability and experience to come up with new ideas that you might not have thought of on your own.

Here are some other ideas that can make you and your organization more inclusive:

Leave No One on the Bench: As a result of the still-recovering global economy, most corporations and other organizations have learned to do more with fewer people. This is why world employment figures are down in most countries, most notably in European countries such as Greece, Italy, and Spain, where unemployment rates are an eye-popping 25 percent, and twice that for younger demographic groups. As a result, today's companies are far leaner than they were just a decade ago. Therefore, you must make sure that every person you are responsible for in your organization is a high-level performer. In order to achieve that, your people need as much information as possible. For example, in the publishing world, I know of several companies that include assistants in every publishing meeting. This has multiple advantages: First, it makes everyone feel included, which helps with morale. At the same time, it further educates these assistants in the business of book publishing, which makes it far more likely that at least some of them will earn promotions down the line. Last, it provides the leaders of these organizations with viewpoints that they would never have in a closed-off, "managers only" meeting. CEOs and other top managers should also reach out to the members of the organization at the lowest level of the hierarchy, so boardroom strategizing isn't divorced from showroom work.

○ *Put Together Your Own Decision-Making Panel:* Why should only CEOs have a board of directors? If you are a leader, you could use the best possible advice from the most diverse group possible. Whether you establish this group in a formal or an informal manner, the key is empowering people to speak their minds when called upon. Convene this panel on a regular basis, and always have a few key items on the agenda ahead of time so your "consultants" have some time to ponder these issues in advance. Next, in order to make sure that you are not leaving out any important topics, ask each member of the group to bring in two or three bullet points that they think require your attention. This way, you develop a two-way mode of communication with this group. And last, take another page from Francis's book by keeping yes-men off the panel; do not be afraid to replace some of these people over time.

○ *Consider an Annual Meeting or Conference for Your Customers and Suppliers:* I have seen this done very successfully by certain companies and organizations. Your customers and your suppliers are two key constituencies that are obviously pivotal to your business. Think of different venues that you can hold for both of them, or one at a time. It can be something as simple as a lunch for your most important customers, or it could be a two-day conference for both suppliers and customers combined. If you do opt for the latter, make sure you have a solid group of people who can pull the event together. Emphasize productivity over perks; the event should be enjoyable, but your priority should be to make deeper connections with your partners, customers, and suppliers. Logistics, agendas, and the like take some time, so make sure to give yourself and your colleagues enough time to bring off the event as flawlessly as possible.

CHAPTER 6

Avoid Insularity

This chapter tackles inclusiveness from a different angle. An institution that is open to people of all walks of life and reaches out to help people of all stripes, wherever they are, cannot be insular.

Over the years, the word *insular* has been associated with many large institutions for obvious reasons. In the case of the Catholic Church, its doctrine has not changed significantly over the centuries, and many use this as ammunition to accuse the Church of being out of touch. While Vatican II made strides toward making mass more appealing—such as no longer giving the liturgy in Latin and turning the altar toward the congregation—there were no fundamental changes in values that made the Church more accessible to outsiders. But, in addition to the Catholic Church, many large organizations and multinational corporations have also been labeled as insular.

Bergoglio wrote extensively about the concept of insularity, though he has not used that specific word. Before we talk about Francis's take, however, let's look at a construct that is closely related to insularity—what has been dubbed the "not-invented-here syndrome." According to management authors Nicholas Webb and Chris Thoen, "not invented here" (or NIH) is defined as follows:

> *[NIH] is the philosophy of social, corporate, or institutional cultures that avoid using or buying already existing products,*

research, standards, or knowledge because of their external
origins and costs. The reasons for not wanting to use the work
of others are varied, but can include fear through lack of
understanding, an unwillingness to value the work of others,
or forming part of a wider "turf war."

Put more succinctly, insular organizations—and NIH institutions—almost always have one thing in common: a certain arrogance that involves the mindset that encompasses an attitude that says, "We have all the answers." Or, alternatively, "If we did not invent it, then it is not worth looking into it—or knowing about it."

There is one multinational company most closely associated with NIH, and that is General Electric, the last remaining company from the list of original Dow stocks (created by Charles Dow in 1896). For many years, GE ranked near the top of the list of *Fortune* magazine's Most Admired Companies in the world; in recent years, however, the company lost some of its luster for a multitude of reasons (including a stock swoon that sent its shares nose-diving to less than $6 per share in the 2008–9 financial crisis).

Yet in the 1960s and 1970s, General Electric was all over the pages of the textbooks and casebooks of the best business schools. That's because its model organization, consisting of dozens of "strategic business units," was thought to be among the best-managed companies in the world.

However, all that attention ultimately had a negative effect on the company. The great press it garnered created a corporation permeated by NIH (according to many, GE invented NIH). "We are General Electric; we don't need any help," thought many GE executives and managers. As a result, by the 1970s, the company had become a bloated bureaucracy and a conglomerate—a collection of businesses that had little to do with each other. It had become an insular organization. (Only by promoting Jack Welch—the man who would later be crowned Manager of the Century by *Fortune* magazine—did the company finally rid itself of NIH and regain its former luster.)

✤ DIALOGUE IS KEY TO TEARING DOWN WALLS

One way to make sure that you do not come down with NIH syndrome is to consult and speak with a great variety of people, especially those who have a different perspective than your own. You should be talking to people inside and outside of your organization, ideally from different parts of the country and around the globe.

As pointed out in Chapter 5, Francis established a counseling body consisting of eight cardinals from all over the world, the so-labeled V-8. Assembling this council shows that he understands intuitively how important it is to get input from various voices. But establishing a consultative group that meets a few times a year is only part of the solution. Another key aspect of avoiding NIH and insularity involves engaging people of all religions and creeds and socioeconomic backgrounds in dialogue, as discussed in Chapter 1.

Few leaders have written as much about the importance of dialogue as Jorge Mario Bergoglio (and I am not the only writer to take note of it). Here, journalist Annemarie C. Mayer sums up Francis's progress on dialogue in an article she authored for a well-respected international Christian journal:

> With Pope Francis a new phase of dialogue seems to have
> begun. He already has considerable experience in dialogue
> with Jews and Muslims. In 2011 he published a book
> entitled Sobre el cielo y la tierra *which means "On Heaven
> and Earth" but also "all and sundry," co-written with*

*Rabbi Abraham Skorka, the rector of the Latin-American
Rabbinical Seminar in Buenos Aires. The co-authors
demonstrate what they mean by inter-religious dialogue. The
aim for all parties engaged in it is to learn from one another.*

Bergoglio has explained that true dialogue can take place only
when each party respects the other individual and approaches the
other as if he or she has something important and pertinent to say,
with the intent to listen as much as to talk. This again speaks to
Francis's foundational roots of respect, dignity, and humility before
oneself, others, and God.

✦ LEAD LIKE AN AUTHENTIC PROPHET

Three years before becoming Pope Francis, Bergoglio wrote extensively about the importance of working with others to achieve
important goals. He felt strongly that only the most narcissistic
among us think that they have all the answers. Explains Bergoglio,
"When someone is self-sufficient, when he has the answers to every
question, it is proof that God is not with him. Self-sufficiency is evi-
dent in every false prophet, in the misguided religious leaders that
use religion for their own ego."

However, Bergoglio does not stop there. As the well-rounded
theologian that he is, he looks to the Old Testament to explain why
we should all "lead like Moses":

*The great leaders of the people of God were men that left
room for doubt. Going back to Moses, he is the most humble
character that there was on Earth. Before God, no one else
remained more humble, and he that wants to be a leader of the
people of God has to give God his space; therefore to shrink,*

to recede into oneself with doubt, with the interior experiences of darkness, of not knowing what to do, all that ultimately is very purifying. The bad leader is the one who is self-assured and stubborn. One of the characteristics of a bad leader is to be excessively normative because of his self-assurance.

This sentiment is strikingly counterintuitive. How many times in today's society do we hear how important confidence is to winning? I am sure there has never been a halftime speech by a football or basketball coach who told his team to be "filled with doubt." Yet that is what Bergoglio is saying here. It is not because he wants his flock to fall short of their goals or dreams, but because through doubt and difficult times (i.e., "interior experiences of darkness") one grows as a human being and a leader. It is not only acceptable to be filled with doubt; it makes you a purer, more humble leader, likely to reach out for help when you need it most.

This is the heart of Francis on full display. And you do not have to be a practicing Christian, or even believe in God, to be great, argues Bergoglio. "I know more agnostic people than atheists; the first are more uncertain, the second are more convinced. [E]very man is the image of God, whether he is a believer or not. For that reason alone everyone has a series of virtues, qualities, and a greatness of his own. If he has some vileness, as I do, we can share that in order to mutually help one another and overcome it."

✤ BERGOGLIO ON BERGOGLIO

One would not expect that a pope would be "filled with doubt" or have "experiences of darkness." Yet, time and again, this pontiff shows us his vulnerable, human side.

Moments after being elected pope, he did more than one thing that was unprecedented. On top of the unexpected actions already discussed in this book, no one could have anticipated what he asked of the people around him in the moments before he stepped out in front of the tens of thousands assembled to greet their new pope at St. Peter's Square.

Francis describes the unusual request he made at that moment: "And now I would like to give the blessing, but first—first I ask a favor of you: before the Bishop blesses his people, *I ask you to pray to the Lord that he will bless me* [italics mine]: the prayer of the people asking the blessing for their Bishop. Let us make, in silence, this prayer: your prayer over me. . . . Now I will give the Blessing to you and the whole world, to all men and women of good will."

How rare it is for a leader, especially the leader of 1.2 billion people and one of the world's oldest institutions, to ask *others* to pray for *him*. Yet Francis did not hesitate for a moment. Some might have felt that this action showed weakness and vulnerability. But in Francis's paradigm, in putting his vulnerability and doubt on full display he was living up to his own expectation of humility before the people and God.

Here, Francis's friend and coauthor of the aforementioned book *On Heaven and Earth*, Rabbi Abraham Skorka, echoes the pope's sentiments on what constitutes an effective leader. "Any religious leader that is prideful and lacks humility, who talks arrogantly and in absolutes, is not a good religious leader. A leader who is arrogant, who does not know how to deal with people, who repeatedly says, '*I am*,' should not be a religious leader."

What additional steps can you take to guard against insularity? Consider these potential actions:

⬮ *Eliminate Insularity* Within *Your Own Organization:*
This is a very important imperative. It is bad enough to be too

inward looking and not know what is happening in the outside
world and the markets in which your firm operates. It may be
worse for departments within your own organization to be so
insular that your people don't even know what their colleagues
down the hall are doing. We have all heard stories of friction
and turf wars between departments in an organization, such as
sales and marketing or marketing and manufacturing. In years
past, these inward-looking divisions have been called *silos*. To
help prevent silo-like thinking and behavior in your firm, host
informal lunches that bring two or more departments together.
Follow that up with off-site meetings involving key players
from all departments. Remember, the key is getting all of your
people on the same page, reading off the same "sheet of music."
Giving all of your people a greater understanding of what their
colleagues contribute to the organization is your best chance of
eliminating inward-focused insularity.

*To Eliminate NIH, Encourage Managers and Employees
Alike to Find a Better Way:* In many organizations, people
hear that competitor X does things so much better than we do.
While I am in no way suggesting that people steal company
secrets, you must ask your people to improve on their best
practices. For example, consider how smartphones moved
almost exclusively to touch screens immediately following the
release of the iPhone. With today's web and other technologies
it is much easier to find out what your rivals are doing, and
how they are doing it. Francis said, ". . . those who stubbornly
try to recover a past that no longer exists . . . have a static and
inward-directed view of things." Do not try to reach back to
the past for ideas that worked for your company. Today's world

changes at such a rapid pace that now you must look to the future for solutions.

⬭ *Invite Another Leader from a Competitor or a Related Industry to Speak to Your People:* This would have been an unthinkable premise two decades ago. But today many companies are involved in sharing best practices with other firms. If you are in a position to invite the CEO of a not-so-direct competitor, do so. And offer the same opportunity to them in return.

CHAPTER 7

Choose Pragmatism
over Ideology

This leadership lesson may be the most counterintuitive of all, especially when we are discussing a pope, but it's the reason behind Pope Francis's consistent inclusiveness.

Throughout his writing and speaking, the pope calls on other leaders to see things individually and based on their own merits. In the journal *El Jesuita*, Francis is quoted as saying, "I don't have all the answers; I don't even have all the questions, and there are always new questions coming forward. But the answers have to be thought out according to the different situations, and you also have to wait for them . . ."

Francis urges religious leaders to do whatever is necessary (within the bounds of ethics) to help one person at a time. And if, in doing so, the leader has to get into the metaphorical—or literal—mud, so much the better.

In 2010, Bergoglio told this story: "I do not have any doubt that we must get our hands dirty. Today, priests no longer wear their cassocks. But a recently ordained priest used to do it and some other priests criticized him. So he asked a wise priest, 'Is it wrong that I wear my cassock?' The problem is not if you wear a cassock or not, but rather if you roll up its sleeves when you have to work for the good of others."

Later, as Francis, in his most frequently quoted homily, he spoke to the Church as a whole: "Here I repeat . . . what I have often said to the priests and laity of Buenos Aires: I prefer a Church which is bruised, hurting, and dirty because it has been out on the streets, rather than a Church which is unhealthy from being confined and from clinging to its own security. I do not want a Church concerned with being at the center and which then ends by being caught in a web of obsessions and procedures."

✦ THE PRAGMATIC POPE

This pope sees things exactly as they are and not how he wishes them to be. As was discussed in the last chapter, the pontiff has taken a number of steps to guard against insularity. Part of that effort is an acknowledgment that the world is not only changing but changing too fast for a huge institution like the Catholic Church to keep up with. However, the Church and its leaders must do their best to change with it; it is unacceptable to force a millennia-old standard on a world that is in an increasingly rapid state of metamorphosis.

Even before he became pontiff, Bergoglio acknowledged the limits of the Catholic Church in responding to a new world: "I admit that the tempo cannot keep up with the speed of social change, but holy leaders, those that seek the voice of God, have to take the necessary time to find the answers. Nevertheless there is the risk of confusing other economic, cultural, and geopolitical interests. It is important to know how to distinguish." Francis is not only a pragmatist but also a realist. Even the loftiest and most well-intentioned ideals will not yield prosperity if they defy reality. Pope Francis does not want to change the Catholic Church's core values; he simply wants to update its operating system to be compatible with the world's ever-evolving networks.

As pontiff, Francis addressed the same issue of change. "If the Christian . . . wants everything clear and safe, then he will find nothing. Tradition and memory of the past must help us to have courage to open up new areas."

"The courage to open up new areas" sounds so simple, yet so many organizations fail because their leaders get stuck in the past, clinging to the old ways that used to work, afraid to face the future, and, thus, unable to devise a new strategic vision for their companies. That's happened to some corporations that once were among the world's most successful.

In his book *Only the Paranoid Survive*, legendary Intel cofounder and former CEO Andy Grove describes something called a *strategic inflection point* (SIP). An SIP is a ten-times force—that is, a change or "disruptive technology" that is ten times as powerful as any change that preceded it. For Intel, the SIP was competition from Japanese memory chips, which were cheaper and more powerful and, as a result, brutalized their core market in the mid-1980s. Only when Grove realized that Intel had to abandon its core product and come up with something new—microprocessors—did the company put itself on a path to become first in its market once again.

It should be noted, however, that Intel's transition was not without pain. One third of the company's workforce had to be laid off, and the reinvention of the company did not just happen overnight.

For Disney, the SIP was the death of its founder in 1966. The company almost went out of business because the people left in charge were afraid to do anything new, subjecting every decision to the test "What Would Walt Do?" It took a new CEO, Michael Eisner, an outsider from Paramount, to reinvent "the house that Walt built."

Today there are many companies facing possible demise because their senior management teams simply assumed that the products that catapulted their firms to stunning success would continue to do so. One of the most noteworthy is BlackBerry. Once the king of mobile devices, with its now famous (or perhaps infamous) keyboards, the company has recently been crushed by companies like Apple and Samsung, thanks to their smartphones.

For BlackBerry, unlike Disney and Intel, it will be nearly impossible to ever regain its leading place in the market. In fact, the firm's current biggest battle is not to climb back to number one but simply to stay in business. Unless it is able to be pragmatic, change, and become relevant again, it is unlikely BlackBerry will succeed.

✧ A PRAGMATIST ON THE FRONTIER

Francis shows his pragmatism in many ways as the leader of the Catholic Church. He understands and acknowledges that the world is a huge, diverse place and that the church's SIP is many cultures' quickly evolving definitions of the "new normal"—from nontraditional marriages and unions to technology's increasing role in everyday life, and to greater emphasis on ecological issues. And he knows that if he is going to fulfill his goal of a more open and welcoming Church, then he must break with the most severe and steadfast parts of Church doctrine by considering changes to things that would have been unfathomable under Benedict XVI or any previous pope, such as allowing civil unions, tolerating divorce, and not judging people on their sexual orientation.

There is another group of people whom Francis admires, and

this one has nothing to do with social stratifications such as marital status or sexual preference. These are special people who go beyond the call of duty, day in and day out, because they live on what Francis has described as the "frontier."

Here, Bergoglio uses a very personal example to explain the term: "The frontiers are many. Let us think of the religious sisters living in hospitals. They live on the frontier. I am alive because of one of them. When I went through my lung disease at the hospital, the doctor gave me penicillin and streptomycin in certain doses. The sister who was on duty tripled my doses because she was daringly astute; she knew what to do because she was with ill people all day. The doctor, who really was a good one, lived in his laboratory. The sister lived on the frontier and was in dialogue with it every day." You can't lead from the back, Francis is saying. You have to lead from the front, where the struggle doesn't end just because the leader has left. So he lives on the frontier himself.

To do so, one must be "audacious" (another favorite Francis word) and courageous. Biographer Paul Vallely commented, "Certainly Bergoglio in all phases of his life has been a shrewd politician, but there has been more to that than sheer ambition. Throughout his career Bergoglio has shown significant courage. . . . There were repeated examples of his personal bravery smuggling out victims of the military dictatorship, standing up to the drug gangs in the slums, and sticking to his principles on interfaith dialogue despite accusations of heresy, apostasy, and disloyalty by ultra-traditionalists in Argentina and Rome. . . . At the same time it is clear that his decision to embrace radical humility was something of a struggle against his own personality with its dogmatic and authoritarian streaks."

What can you do to be more pragmatic and rely less on ideology? Consider these ideas:

Pragmatism Starts with a Mindset: Pragmatists see the world for what it is, not how they wish it to be. As humble as Pope Francis is, he describes himself as a "political animal." He knew that to become the 266th pontiff, he would have to understand the politics of the conclave, even though he was too humble to actually campaign for the job in any covert manner. Likewise, Francis urges people to engage in office politics, because he is a pragmatist and knows that those people who do not engage in the underlying culture or politics of an organization will be left behind. Rather than avoid office politics, which albeit are frequently a waste of time—or, worse, spending your time instead wishing you lived in a world without them—participate, but don't succumb. Use the dramas as a way to demonstrate your own leadership skills by solving problems, bringing antagonists together and turning them into teams, and creating a more collegial atmosphere instead of a poisonous one. You may have to be ruthless and get rid of those who would root for the poison, but most people don't like office politics and they'll be glad to see the snakes banished, too.

Open Up New Areas: Pope Francis urges people to chart new paths in their field of endeavor. Experimenting with new ideas and products or services is certainly consistent with a pragmatist's view of the world. That's because the pragmatist knows that one day something that worked well for an individual or organization won't work anymore. Intel's founders learned that the hard way, which is why its cofounder Andy Grove urges managers to always be experimenting with new ideas and products. Evaluating new processes can also help your company keep up with trends. Make sure your procedures are as efficient as possible by assessing work flow and deciding whether new technologies can be implemented to make your time go further.

- *Live on the Frontier:* Although *frontier*—or *new frontier*— were popular words and phrases for John F. Kennedy when he campaigned for president, Francis has a slightly different meaning for the word today. In American parlance, he means pushing the envelope by doing courageous things on the front lines. Don't be afraid to push yourself beyond limits that are self-imposed or placed on you by society or convention; you might be surprised what you can accomplish if you do things Francis's way.

CHAPTER 8

Employ the Optics of Decision Making

D ecision making is such a vital leadership topic because it touches upon several other leadership characteristics, such as establishing priorities and leading by example. Decision making is also one of Pope Francis's favorite topics. He has often discussed his decision making throughout his career, including his own approaches to decisions and how his technique has evolved. If we cannot quite discern a complete arc of his evolution on the topic, we can at least get a good idea of how he "course-corrected" and refined his decision-making methods over the years.

✦ THE POLITICS OF DECISION MAKING

Francis has long believed that he is not at all immune to politics. As we have discussed, it is his pragmatic side that allows him to see the politics of his position. He has a firm grip on what motivates leaders—and that includes himself as well. He said in 2010, "We are all Political animals with a capital 'P.' . . . [T]he preaching of human and religious values has a political consequence."

He understood that his role was as political as it was spiritual;

however, Bergoglio (as he was known at the time) also added, "Something has happened to our politics, it is out of ideas, out of proposals. . . . They have shifted ideas of political platforms to aesthetic ideas. Today, image is more important than what is proposed. Plato said it in *The Republic*, rhetoric—which equals aesthetics—is to politics what cosmetics is to health. We have displaced the essential with the aesthetic; we have deified polling and marketing."

So making snap decisions in today's political world has severe consequences. *How* leaders decide is as significant as *what* leaders decide; they must reflect their policy in their decision-making process. Never mind that there are many leaders in politics and business who boast of their "gut" decision-making prowess; Francis feels that the decisions he made like this were impetuous and that his leadership suffered as a result. The impulsive decisions the younger Bergoglio made had two negative effects: First, such decision making underscored his immaturity as a leader, and, second, it caused others to mislabel him as an ultraconservative.

Francis has also learned that making key decisions without consulting with others was another flaw in his method. This need for counsel speaks again to Francis's inclusivity. Hence, he enacts his policy in his decision making.

✦ DECIDING TO BE HUMBLE

Bergoglio's statement about politics, cited in the previous section, explains much about his first moves as Pope Francis. The humble way he presented himself to the world was a series of carefully made decisions. Likewise, his decision to take a public bus, rather than the papal motorcade, to return to the hotel in which he was staying also speaks volumes about Francis's instincts. (The reason Francis decided to return to the hotel personally was so that he could pay the balance on his bill himself.)

Journalist Michael Terheyden, writing about Francis's "True Leadership," asserts that it was also noteworthy that the newly elected pope chose to maintain his old motto, "lowly but chosen," and that Francis has lived up to it ever since.

Were all these decisions made because of the aesthetics, or what are also called the "optics," of the situation? Of course, but that does not mean that Francis has not been sincere. By the time Bergoglio became Francis, he had learned to be the most humble of leaders, and he has eschewed just about anything that is not also accessible to his flock.

Some people close to the pontiff feel that his decision to be humble was indeed a conscious one and came to him only after many humbling years in the slums. Rabbi Abraham Skorka explained that Francis is not faking it, but that he made a deliberate decision to be humble and worked at it with much fervor.

Biographer Paul Vallely agrees that humility was not Francis's most natural path. "It is clear that his decision to embrace radical humility was something of a struggle against his own personality with its dogmatic and authoritarian streaks." Vallely's comments on a "dogmatic" and "authoritarian" Francis match up with Francis's own assessment of himself as a younger Jesuit leader.

By the time Bergoglio became Francis, he knew how to play politics as cannily as any of his peers. He also understood how optics could be used to transform the papacy, by living humbly, in order to be as close to his flock as his new position allowed.

So how did Francis transition from the impulsive to the discerning decider? Like any wise leader, he learned from experience. Those impulsive decisions made in his younger days were not his best, and he admitted it in a 2013 interview, in which he chastises himself for his earlier manner of rushed decision making. "I am always wary of the first decision, that is, the first thing that comes to my mind if I have to make a decision. This is usually the wrong thing. I have to wait and assess, looking deep into myself, taking the necessary time. The wisdom of discernment redeems the necessary ambiguity of life and helps us find the most appropriate means, which do not always coincide with what looks great and strong."

❖ MAKE PEOPLE-DECISIONS YOUR PRIORITY

According to leadership experts Noel Tichy and Warren Bennis, authors of the book *Judgment: How Winning Leaders Make Great Calls*, selecting leaders is the single most important task of other leaders. "Good people-judgment calls require that it [hiring top people] be the [leader's] most important agenda." Although Tichy and Bennis were specifically talking about hiring heads of corporations and other institutions (e.g., CEOs), there are decisions about secondary hires that are nearly as important as the decisions you make when hiring the person at the top of an organization. More often than not, it is the number two person that is called upon to execute on the vision of the organization's leader.

When Michael Eisner nabbed the top spot as chairman and CEO of Disney in 1984, he and other Disney executives insisted on bringing in a number two person to help reinvent the company, which was in trouble. Like Francis's deliberate decisions, Eisner's move to hire a second in command filled a need at Disney, but it also sent a message. He did not want to set himself up as the next Walt—if he did, the company would just crumble again upon his departure. So the hiring of Frank Wells signaled the reinvention of Disney in its management structure as well as its outlook for the future.

The decision of *whom* to hire also speaks to the significance in the choice. This person would have to be on board with Eisner's goal to breathe new life into the company. So before this number two person could even be hired, Eisner had to be deliberate in his own strategy to be able to find someone who could complement it and execute it. That individual was Wells, who served as president and chief operating officer (from 1984–93). Wells ultimately played a pivotal role in helping Eisner fulfill his goal. He was often the one who executed on the vision of Eisner, whether it was creating a new movie studio (e.g., Touchstone) or opening a new overseas theme park. When Wells died in an accident in 1994, Disney faltered again because he had been the stabilizing force that kept so many different minds working with synergy. Ultimately, the loss of Wells led to Eisner's downfall; Wells had been such an integral choice as second in command that Eisner could not recover.

Francis also faced the choice of whom to hire for his second in command. After being elected by the papal conclave, Francis had to choose his secretary of state. Journalist John Allen weighed in for the *National Catholic Reporter* in 2013 on the significance of this position: "In a small world such as the Vatican, personnel is always policy. Nothing says more about where a pope wants to go than the people he chooses to help get him there, and pride of place in that mix generally goes to the Secretary of State, by tradition a pope's 'Prime Minister.'" That article was published immediately after Francis appointed Pietro Parolin to the position at the end of August 2013.

Francis revealed in an interview that he selected Parolin just four days after the conclave, but he kept the decision to himself until the end of August—five and a half months later. The speed of the selection Francis made seems to go against his own, self-described decision-making method (remember—he said that his first choice is almost always the wrong one). Yet here we find the exception that proves the rule. While Francis privately chose Parolin quickly, it is that five-and-a-half-month interval that shows the maturity of his decision making. Though Francis does not always trust his first instinct, he does not allow this mistrust to rule it out completely. And the time he waited between deciding and announcing his decision gave him the opportunity to reflect on and analyze his choice.

Pope Francis offered Parolin the job by phone, and he asked the following question: "Do you want to help me?"

Parolin unflinchingly answered, "Yes."

After announcing Parolin as his secretary of state, members of the media practically fell over themselves to praise the appointment. Gianni Valente, writing for the *Vatican Insider,* pointed out the natural fit between Pope Francis and his new secretary of state. "Parolin's temperament suggests that as Vatican secretary of state he will try to take different ecclesiastical sensitivities into account, countering that self-referential aspect of the Church that Francis has always spoken out against. In the true spirit of Vatican diplomacy, Parolin has always been realistic, carefully studying contexts and problems that need to be solved and searching for possible solutions. . . . Following Francis's path of pastoral conversion, Vatican diplomacy will be able to offer a creative contribution to Church action, inspired by the Bishop of Rome's invitation to come out of itself and go out to men and women in the geographical and existential peripheries in which they live."

While that is an apt description of precisely what Parolin can do to assist Francis, it is likely journalist Massimo Franco who summed up Parolin's new role most astutely: "It may be Francis's nomination of a new secretary of state for the Vatican—a role to be significantly rebranded as 'papal secretary'—that should be viewed as the true *turning point* of his pontificate. The appointment of Monsignor

Pietro Parolin . . . transformed the image of the office and coincided with the Holy See's return to the international scene after the inertia of Benedict XVI's foreign policy."

Parolin has an incredible résumé, but he is seen as a Vatican insider. He served the Holy See for two decades as a diplomat and several additional years as in the nunciatures of Nigeria and Mexico. These three decades of service are why some pundits concluded erroneously that the choice of Parolin was evidence that Francis would not seek to reinvent the papacy but instead would simply go down the road already paved by Cardinal Ratzinger/Pope Benedict XVI.

In fact, the choice of Parolin proves quite the opposite. Francis wants to bring about radical change in an institution with the most entrenched bureaucracy in the world, so he needs someone to help him navigate the very difficult waters *inside* the Vatican. Upon his election Francis was a Vatican outsider, but he was not naïve enough to believe that he could execute on his "inclusivity doctrine" without someone who was intimately familiar with the nuances of the insular Vatican.

Furthermore, in elevating Parolin, Francis was actually making a two-pronged decision: In promoting Parolin to the number two spot, the pontiff had to dismiss the controversial Cardinal Tarcisio Bertone, who served under Pope Benedict XVI. According to the Religion News Service, "Bertone has been accused of not doing enough to address the scandals and crisis that marred Benedict's pontificate, from the sex abuse scandal to the rehabilitation of a Holocaust-denying traditionalist bishop, up to the so-called Vatileaks scandal." The decision to oust Bertone was Francis's way of saying that he would not tolerate sweeping these problems under the rug. Thus, this decision, while a necessary action to be able to appoint Parolin, was, in fact, a statement in itself.

Finally, in tapping Parolin, Francis gave his stamp of approval to a figure very close to himself in his humility. Parolin said when he learned of his appointment, "Above all, I feel the full weight of the responsibility placed upon me: this call entrusts to me a difficult and challenging mission, before which my powers are weak and my abilities poor." The last part of that excerpt echoes the humility doctrine that Francis espouses.

It is still early days for Parolin in his new role. However, he is prepared to reform the Church and the Curia alongside Francis. "I really hope there will be a real reform of the spirit," declared Parolin in December 2013. "The important thing is for all of us to renew ourselves in order to be in a continual conversion." Above all, Parolin stands as a symbolic testament to Francis's wisdom and awareness of the optics of choice.

How can you improve your decision-making prowess? Consider the following ideas:

- *Always Put People-Decisions at the Top of Your To-Do List:* People-decisions are the most important decisions any leader can make. The cost of a bad hire is sometimes incalculable, since the opportunity cost is always high, and the effort required to remove a person is often very arduous. When hiring your number two, think not only of what he or she needs to do for you, but what your role would be like without the person. At Disney, Eisner floundered after Wells's death; while you do not want to be so reliant on your second in command that the person's departure would be your ruin, you do want someone who can facilitate for you what you cannot. It is not only in Francis's world that people come first; if you lead people, then they are your top priority as well.

● *Do Not Rush Key Decisions:* Even though Francis made a
  quick calculation to hire Pietro Parolin as his secretary of state,
  he advocates taking his time with all decisions. To Francis,
  it is not about trusting your gut; instead, it is about taking all
  the time you need to reason through a number of different
  scenarios before pulling the trigger on any one course of action.
  Furthermore, a decision is never "over" once you have reached
  your verdict. A truly successful leader continually evaluates his
  or her decisions and makes adjustments as needed.

● *Make Decisions That Advance Your Strategy:* Pope Francis
  has made a number of statements and decisions geared to
  advance his goal of making the Catholic Church a far more
  accepting institution. When making any decision, take the time
  to think through the various outcomes: Is this a decision that
  harmonizes with my strategic plan? If not, you may want to
  hold off and think through a number of alternative scenarios.
  Furthermore, understand the optics of your decision making.
  Ask yourself what the decision will say. If you don't know, seek
  feedback from people you trust.

CHAPTER 9

Run Your Organization Like
a Field Hospital

ope Francis has a unique perspective on the Catholic Church.
He likes to compare it to a mobile army surgical hospital
(MASH) unit, or a field hospital—a temporary hospital set up close
to a battle zone to provide emergency care for the wounded. He said
in 2013, "The thing the church needs most today is the ability to
heal wounds and to warm the hearts of the faithful: it needs nearness, proximity. I see the church as a field hospital after battle. It is
useless to ask a seriously injured person if he has high cholesterol
and about the level of his blood sugars! You have to heal his wounds.
Then we can talk about everything else. Heal the wounds, heal the
wounds . . . and you have to start from the ground up."

Francis's allusion, while seeming at first almost like a non sequi-
tur, actually meshes completely with the rest of his philosophy that
we have come to know. A MASH unit allows the doctors to smell
like their flock (Chapter 2). A field hospital is certainly inclusive, not
turning anyone away in need of care (Chapter 5). By definition, a field
hospital cannot be insular, since it goes to the battlefield where the
wounded lie, waiting to see a doctor or surgeon (Chapter 6). And the
nature of the emergency care given to the wounded leaves no time to
judge the victims for their injuries (Chapter 3).

Francis does not want members of the clergy to see the Church as some prim and genteel institution with a pristine façade. On the contrary—he would rather see an institution battle-scarred from the hands-on service it gives to its flock. Only then can a leader of the Church claim he has done everything he can to help the people—all people, believers and nonbelievers alike, regardless of sexual orientation, marital status, and so on. After all, a field hospital after battle accepts everyone in need of attention.

The one difference in Francis's portrayal of a field hospital is that not only do his "medics" take care of the physically injured; in a Francis MASH unit, the leaders attend to the wounds of the soul. The pragmatic Francis understands that the people in greatest need of the Church are spiritually wounded. And everyday life often brings many of the most common problems, whether they be financial difficulties, relationship issues, the loss of a loved one, or the loss of a job or career. More specifically, the problem may be someone facing a gut-wrenching divorce that leaves the person psychologically wounded, or a loving father involved in a nasty custody battle who tries to find understanding and forgiveness in his situation, or a gay teenager ridiculed and bullied at school who searches for answers and comfort. Francis lives among all of these people. He understands their pain and wants other leaders of the church to tend to all members of their flocks and do whatever they can to help them heal. If they don't come to church, then you must go to them, urges Pope Francis. That is the duty of anyone who is responsible for leading other people.

When you look at the patients in Francis's field hospital in those terms—as people who have been wounded by the harsh realities of life—several of the pontiff's leadership values and tenets come together. One is his sense of urgency. He does not believe in helping the poor and less fortunate tomorrow when we can help them today.

"How are we treating the people of God? I dream of a church that is a mother and shepherdess. The church's ministers must be merciful, take responsibility for the people and accompany them like the good Samaritan, who washes, cleans, and raises up his neighbor. . . . The structural and organizational reforms are secondary—that is, they come afterward." Francis is urging his clergy to offer solace to the soul before anything and everything else. It is always the people and their wounds that come first.

Francis also believes the youth in our society have a priority over the rest of other members of the flock. When it comes to the young up-and-comers in the Church, he speaks of the need for serious and sincere dialogue. "We must form their hearts," he said. "Otherwise we are creating little monsters." In training young priests, Francis, who before his time as pope was the head of the Jesuits' novice training program in Argentina, believes that the focus should move from rigorous and meditative ritual to cultivation of compassion and activism. He said, "Truly to understand reality we need to move away from the central position of calmness and peacefulness and direct ourselves to the peripheral areas." Rather than create "administrators," concluded Francis, we must focus on creating a generation of "fathers, brothers, and traveling companions."

✦ HOW A MASH UNIT WORKS FOR BUSINESS

Francis's field-hospital metaphor works well for most any type of organization or business. First, in this hypercompetitive age, you must adopt the great sense of urgency associated with a MASH unit. Companies that sit on their product lead, especially in the technology arena, find themselves run over by the competition. Earlier we described what happened to BlackBerry: It went from being the market leader in handheld devices to a company that is fighting a losing battle to remain relevant.

The other great benefit associated with a field hospital is that it is portable and nimble—it can go wherever it is needed, and it can pick up and move with great agility when conditions on the ground necessitate it. Imagine if your organization had that ability. Let's say your firm was courting a new customer located across the country. Wouldn't it be helpful if you could temporarily move your company right next to that customer's location? Of course, you cannot move your entire company. But you *can* put together a "Go Team" that visits that customer twice a month. In this age of Skype, e-mails, digital conferencing, and social media, there are not enough face-to-face meetings taking place between key people in an organization and customers and potential customers. There is still no substitute for pressing the flesh and getting to know your customers on a first-name, "it is great to see you again" basis.

However, the biggest lesson businesspeople can learn from the MASH unit is that it operates independently. Sure, it is in touch with other parts of the service corps, but it does not call some sort of head office to get permission to treat a chest wound or a soldier with shrapnel in the leg and abdomen. In that regard, the MASH unit is on its own—it is decentralized. And that is a model that many businesses can learn from.

✥ DECENTRALIZE DECISION MAKING

In the United States in the 1960s and 1970s, large companies like General Motors and General Electric were operated as centralized corporations, in which most key decisions were made by the top managers in the "home office." Things changed in the 1980s, in part because of one of the bestselling business books of all time. In 1982, author and futurist John Naisbitt wrote the bestseller *Megatrends*. That book, which sold an astronomical fourteen million copies, stayed on the *New York Times* Best Sellers list for more than two years. One of the key trends in that book discussed the move from centralization to decentralization. After that, the management textbooks used in business schools made decentralization a key topic in the curriculum.

Pope Francis has come out strongly in favor of decentralization, which is a natural outgrowth of his humility. Why should a self-described sinner like Francis claim that he has all the answers? He is humble enough to admit that he hasn't. He expounded on this issue in his now well-known homily *Evangelii Gaudium*. "Countless issues involving evangelization today might be discussed here, but I have chosen not to explore these many questions, which call for further reflection and study. Nor do I believe that the papal magisterium should be expected to offer a definitive or complete word on every question which affects the Church and the world. It is not advisable for the Pope to take the place of local Bishops in the discernment of every issue which arises in their territory. In this sense, I am conscious of the need to promote a sound 'decentralization.' "

Three years before he penned that homily, Bergoglio wrote, "The teacher who nullifies the decision-making for his disciple is not a good priest; he is a good dictator, denying others their religious personalities." Francis has been able to decentralize because, as discussed in Chapter 8, he makes very strong people-decisions. He is able to hire the best people for the most important assignments and leave them alone to make their own decisions. Pope Francis is a very trusting individual; once he places someone in a position, he assumes that person is doing the job well until that individual proves otherwise.

How can you learn to run your organization more like a field hospital? Consider the following ideas:

- *Make Sure Your People Spend Enough Time in the Field:* Obviously, your organization cannot be transformed into a field hospital. However, that does not mean that your people cannot go out and spend more time in the field with key customers, suppliers, and potential customers. Unless management urges people to travel, they won't. If you cut your travel budget because of lower revenues, you may be cutting off your best way to boost the top and bottom lines.

- *Maintain an Open-Door Policy:* If you are a manager, you are responsible for your "flock," whether you like it or not. Keeping an open-door policy ensures that anyone in need of "care" can see you. In this age in which privacy is such a vital concern, you should not ask your people personal questions about their private lives. But if they are deeply troubled and in need of a confidant(e), you can fill that role if they come to you. Many people see their boss as a source of wisdom and comfort, so offer that if they come to you. Just be careful that you do not go beyond the boundary of the workplace. In other words, if someone comes to you so troubled that you do not know how to help, put the person in touch with specialists that your company is affiliated with.

- *Decentralize Decision Making:* Perhaps you are a type-A personality who likes to make every decision. Well, that does not work anymore. Maybe twenty years ago you could get away with that sort of behavior, but not in the twenty-first century. You need to make sure that you hire—and promote—people who are professional, well trained, and capable of handling their responsibilities. Too much micromanaging takes away from your ability to do your own job, and it shows a lack of trust in your reports. Allow your people to make decisions, and be ready to give support when you are asked.

CHAPTER 10

Live on the Frontier

How is it that a man as humble and self-deprecating as Jorge Mario Bergoglio was elected to the highest office in one of the largest institutions in the world? By all accounts, the Catholic Church is a vast bureaucracy of fiefdoms, pockets of power, and cronyism; yet Bergoglio, who arrived at the conclave with no expectation that he would be elected, had few ties to the powerful cliques in Rome. Bergoglio was a 44-to-1 underdog according to oddsmakers, and he knew it going in. So how did he do it?

Francis lives on the frontier while still exercising power and living by a self-imposed code of radical humility. Recall the Chapter 7 example of the nurse who tripled Bergoglio's prescribed dosage of antibiotics when he was gravely ill. In recalling the episode, Bergoglio wrote, "The sister lived on the frontier and was in dialogue with it every day."

The nurse who saved Bergoglio's life saw how sick he was and knew that he needed more medicine, because she had nursed so many patients and seen so much disease. Francis uses the word *frontier* to mean someone who lives on the periphery, someone who is enough of a nonconformist to make decisions that are unexpected or counterintuitive, but with enough experience to be confident in those decisions. To Francis, the most effective members in the clergy live on the frontier and possess the courage to go out and help anyone in need. Declared Francis, "Wake up the world! Be witness of a different way of doing things, of acting, of living! It is possible to live differently in this world." He added, "You cannot bring home the frontier, but you have to live on the border and be audacious."

Being a humble leader does not prevent Francis from exercising authority and power when needed. He is a three-dimensional leader—far more than a kindly, avuncular figure who only performs humble acts all day. It is his humility, however, that places him on the frontier. He acts with authority, courage, and the wisdom of experience, but he allows room for other ideas, because he knows he cannot possibly have all the answers. Francis biographer Paul Vallely called this the perfect "combination of humility and power" that convinced the cardinals to elevate Bergoglio to pope back in March 2013.

✦ WHERE IS THE FRONTIER?

The frontier is not a place; it is more of a positive and broad-minded attitude coupled with courage and audacity. Living on the frontier means doing different things for different people, depending in large part on what one does for a living (but certainly not restricted to a person's career). For members of the clergy, immersing themselves deeply in the community they serve and going out to help all members of their community is living on the frontier. Observing and judging the problems of their flock from a distance and examining crime statistics is the opposite. Here is how Francis wrote about this phenomenon:

> *When it comes to social issues, it is one thing to have a meeting to study the problem of drugs in a slum neighborhood and quite another to go there, live there, and understand the*

problem from the inside and study it. . . . [O]ne cannot speak
of poverty if one does not experience poverty, with a direct
connection to the places in which there is poverty.

Francis expects that not just his clergy but all people "need to become acquainted with reality by experience, to spend time walking on the periphery in order really to become acquainted with the reality and life experiences of people. If this does not happen, we then run the risk of being abstract ideologists or fundamentalists, which is not healthy."

✢ YOUR FRONTIER

Most of us have lived on the frontier at one time or another. Much depends on what your profession, and your life, offers you, and in turn, what decisions and life choices you make along the way. In most cases, your frontier will not require heroic acts, such as "curing" people of poverty and illness in the slums; most of us can live on the frontier even if we simply have everyday kinds of jobs.

Let's turn to the world of a relatively small business. You are a senior supervisor in the sales department of a growing, profitable food business based in Chicago, Illinois. You manage a team of twelve field salespeople in your district. Your boss, who managed you and three other senior supervisors, recently resigned after accepting a compelling offer from a close competitor. Now there is a vacuum left by your boss's recent departure. Not only was your manager an effective leader, he also handled a handful of the company's key accounts in New York. You really want his job. You think to yourself, "I deserve that job; I have the most seniority—and the best results of the four senior supervisors." You are sure that you are the most qualified for the position. However, you hear through the grapevine that the vice president in charge of your department is thinking of bringing in an outsider to fill that spot. Still, she has not yet made up her mind one way or the other.

What do you do? Do you simply approach the vice president and ask for the management position, laying out your case for "deserving" the promotion (seniority, results, etc.)? That would certainly be audacious, but does it conform to Francis's definition of living on the frontier?

You probably guessed it—the short answer is no. There is an entirely different route you can take that ensures maximum humility and dignity in the workplace while senior managers decide on the best course of action to fill that just-vacated management position.

This sounds counterintuitive, but if you want to proceed the Francis way you have to forget about yourself and getting that promotion, no matter how badly you want that job. Instead, think of what the organization and your colleagues need at that moment in time.

Remember, Bergoglio never asked to be pope—not in 2005 and not in 2013. He left it to *others* to make a case for him (although he did give a compelling three-and-a-half-minute speech at the 2013 conclave—but the talk was not about himself; instead, it was about the needs of the Catholic Church). So we know Francis would not recommend that you storm the VP's office and nakedly campaign for the position. Such an approach lacks humility and gets you nowhere near the frontier. So what would Francis urge you to do?

It all starts with the attitude. You must subordinate your own personal goals and desires. In other words, what you want at this time is not important—it's the organization and its needs that come first. You have to push ambition aside for the time being. That is what Pope Francis has recommended to people in his organization.

When speaking to the Vatican's trainee diplomats, he would warn them against ambition and careerism.

If you want to approach the situation the Francis way, you must face reality and understand that the company has a problem because it has lost a valuable, contributing member of your firm. But you need to be selfless, sincere, and pure at heart as you help guide the company through this difficult period.

So how do you start? The key question to ask at this moment is this: What can I do to help the business grow when we are one person down? As the most senior supervisor in the department, you have a responsibility to put petty politics aside—in your heart and in real, pragmatic ways—as you make your expertise available to your colleagues. You must tread carefully and not be seen as an ambitious and cold opportunist. Instead of being the bull in the china shop, let each of those managers *quietly* know that you are there if and when they need advice or feedback. This low-key approach is just what your colleagues—and the organization—need at this time. In summary, you should do whatever you can to assist your colleagues to perform *their* jobs better.

The next step is a bit more complicated. While you cannot go directly to your VP and tell her you want the job, what about those key accounts that your manager used to handle? They are now in danger of being poached by your old boss or another competitor, so something must be done. This is where nuance matters a great deal.

You do need to approach the VP if she has not approached you yet. However, this impromptu meeting must be handled carefully. You can knock on her door and ask her if she "has a minute." Then quickly state your business. "I know we are a bit shorthanded, and I am somewhat concerned with our New York accounts," you say respectfully yet authoritatively. "So if you need someone to get on a plane to get to the East Coast, just let me know, and I will pack my bags. I'm sure I can get up to speed quickly on each of our key customers since the files are in great shape." If she takes you up on your offer, you begin to approach Francis's frontier. While you might not like New York City, and you don't even like to fly, you have really put yourself out there, far from your Midwest comfort zone, when you volunteered to go to New York and spend some real face time with key customers.

What about your promotion? You cannot even think about it. Your entire focus has to be on retaining and solidifying those New York accounts and making sure that you do not take your eye off the ball of your current responsibilities. You have a full plate. Remember this: In most companies, especially smaller businesses, the most responsible senior managers know what is happening throughout the organization. That is another way of saying that if you do everything you have volunteered to do, and do it well, the chances are good that you will get that promotion. Of course, there are no guarantees in life, and if your company hires from the outside and passes you over for the job, then you may have another decision to make. But in the meantime, live on the frontier in New York, and show them what you are capable of doing. If you do that, the rest of the pieces should fall into place.

What other things can you do to work on the frontier of your industry? Consider the following:

- *"Go There, Live There, and Understand":* If you have the ability to logistically organize your team so that you can be in close contact with them throughout the day, do so. Check in with them on a daily or weekly basis just to know that everything is good in their world. Be intimate with their responsibilities so that you can understand the burdens and stresses in their lives. If you don't know how to use the data entry software that they use, for example, spend some time with it to learn how to speak their language. Be a leader whom they feel they can approach and who will empathize with their issues.

● *Get Out of Your Comfort Zone:* To get to the frontier, you must do things that do not come easily to you. If you could improve your position by getting new clients, but you hate cold calling, then allocate a certain amount of time each week to cold calling and develop a script to work from, refine as you go along, and personalize for each call. If you feel that you don't give feedback to your reports often enough, start scheduling weekly or monthly one-on-one meetings to give them an update. You might not even know what some of your weaknesses are. Ask your manager and your reports for feedback on skills that you can improve. Both will appreciate your faith in them.

● *Help Your Team Join You on the Frontier:* You have learned from Pope Francis's example, so encourage your team to follow your example as well. Pretend that you are, instead of the manager seeking a promotion in the preceding scenario, the vice president. If your employee comes to you looking for an opportunity to grow, and you feel that the person is able to handle the job, allow him or her to take on the responsibility. Don't confine your audacity to your own actions; allow your team to take risks as well, and you can enjoy their successes together.

CHAPTER 11

Confront Adversity Head-On

In late March 2014, Pope Francis knelt down and publicly gave his own confession. This showed the world two things: one, that he is indeed a sinner, as he has often defined himself; and two, that by extension everyone is a sinner, and that it is all right. (According to Catholicism, the only man to ever live without sin was Jesus Christ.) The key is to give confession so that you may be forgiven and continue to strive to live a life of character, dignity, and morality. That a self-described sinner can still hold the highest office in the Catholic Church explains why he is so accepting of so many different kinds of people. Becoming pontiff also speaks to how a flawed figure can overcome his sins and great adversity and still become one of the most respected and popular figures on the world stage.

❖ BERGOGLIO AS PARADOX

Many of the key obstacles in Francis's life came before he was pope; Bergoglio's considerable leadership skills were born out of a life of inner struggles. Bergoglio was 76 years old when he was elected pope. For a society that is, in large part, built for youth, he is an elder statesman. Few of us, if any, in any country, are able to land such an impressive and impactful position at that age. People are usually retired by 75 (if not 65). Yet for his many years, and even though Francis is a man of great wisdom, he still has to battle, for lack of a better phrase, his natural biases and inner conflicts.

Paul Vallely reveals the complexity and paradox of Pope Francis. "Jorge Mario Bergoglio is a doctrinal traditionalist but an ecclesiastical reformer. He is a radical but not a liberal. He seeks to empower others and yet retains a streak of authoritarianism. He is a conservative yet was on the far left of his nation's reactionary Bishop's Conference. He combines religious simplicity with political guile. He is progressive and open, yet austere and severe. . . . He is a teacher of theology but a pastor with the common touch. In him humility and power come together."

This three-dimensional portrait is what makes Francis so compelling. He is like us—capable of complexity and nuance, and has had to overcome obstacles to get to where he is today.

✦ THE BUSY BERGOGLIO BOYHOOD

Pope Francis says that he had a happy childhood, wanting for nothing, even though he had quite a bit to overcome. His mother was paralyzed after the birth of the family's fifth child. That meant that young Bergoglio had to become more self-reliant and cook more of his own meals, a habit that stayed with him for a lifetime (he still cooks meals at his papal apartment at the Casa Santa Marta). But it was his father's plans for him that made his life so complicated.

When he was thirteen years of age, he had enrolled in a rigorous six-year program that would earn him a degree as a chemical technician. He had it all figured out, that is, until his father stunned him by telling him that not only did he have to attend school, but it was also time for him to go to work. So Jorge would attend school from eight o'clock in the morning until one o'clock in the afternoon. Then from 2 p.m. to 8 p.m., he would work in a hosiery factory. First he cleaned, then two years later he did clerical work, and finally he landed a job in a food laboratory. He credits his superb work ethic to the boss he had at the food lab: "She taught me the seriousness of hard work. . . . The work I did was one of the best things I've done in my life. In particular in the laboratory I got to see the good and bad of human endeavor."

If work and school were not enough of a challenge, as a teenager he also had to deal with a serious lung infection, as mentioned earlier. The illness was so bad that one of his lungs had to be removed, though he has never dwelled on this loss as an adult.

Some might face such a series of adversities with a "why me?" attitude. Or they might simply crack under the pressure. Bergoglio has used the stress of competing responsibilities to his advantage, learning from each setback and using them to inform his life. From his mother's problems, he gained independence; from the struggle to balance school and work, he gained discipline; and from his serious illness, he gained perspective on the frontier, which would become the foundation of his philosophy.

To be a truly great leader, you must turn your setbacks into opportunities to grow. Many businesspeople credit a setback as being the cause of their ultimate success. Getting laid off can be an opportunity to reexamine your career and decide that you would rather pursue a new avenue, go back to school, or even start your own business. Having a product fail can force you to look at the development of your next product in a different way. Dwelling on past injuries will not help you in the future. To be a leader of the magnitude of Pope Francis, you have to recognize that sometimes you will falter, and that mistakes are acceptable as long as they can contribute to future triumphs.

✦ TAKING ON THE CHURCH'S GREATEST BATTLE

Let's fast-forward to the current day. There is one topic that has tarnished the Catholic Church for years and confounded Vatican leaders, including Pope Francis. After one full year as pope, Francis still has had a difficult time dealing with the Church sex abuse cases and the press coverage that has ensued, including the disclosure that between 2004 and 2013, 848 priests had been defrocked.

Early on as pontiff, Francis announced a zero-tolerance policy on the sexual abuse and hit all the right notes: "When a priest abuses," asserted Francis, "you must never look away. You cannot be in a position of power and use it to destroy the life of another person."

However, as time went on and Francis approached his first anniversary as pope, the press coverage was more negative than ever. The cable news reports on the sex abuses were blistering. The media insisted that the Vatican was dragging its feet on the matter, by obscuring and allegedly covering up facts. In December 2013 the United Nations issued a report that confirmed everyone's worst fears about the Vatican's mishandling of the matter. The reality was that Pope Francis had not moved quickly enough to deal with the issue.

To exacerbate the matter, Pope Francis made a rare misstep when he told a local newspaper in early 2014, "The Catholic Church is perhaps the lone institution to have moved with transparency and responsibility. No one else has done more. And yet the church is the only one that has been attacked." Those remarks were met with scorn and cynicism, at best. Clyde Haberman of the *New York Times* said, "To some ears, those remarks sounded almost Egan-like in defensiveness." (Cardinal Edward M. Egan is most infamous for denying that he should have ever apologized on behalf of the Catholic Church for the abuses.) Whether he was conscious of it or not, with these words Pope Francis was sidestepping the issue. His comment made it look as if he was either out of the loop or just plain deluded on the topic.

But he was neither. Just before the UN report was released, Pope Francis finally did take some meaningful steps to deal with the scandal in a serious manner. He assembled a commission to provide counsel on the correct protocol for dealing with sex abuse. The makeup of the commission was noteworthy: four of the eight members of the panel were women, including Marie Collins, who, as a thirteen-year-old, was sexually assaulted by a chaplain in Ireland, and who has since become a prominent voice in the fight for accountability in the Church. More than half of the members of the council are not part of the clergy.

Most recently, at the time of the writing of this book, Pope Francis has begun to make amends for not only the Church's wrongdoings, but for his own missteps in the matter. He has recognized that his defensive statement about the Catholic Church's (albeit fruitless) attempts to end the abuses and cover-ups helped no one but the institution itself—the opposite of his intention. On April 11, 2014, Pope Francis stepped up to tackle the issue head-on, in an unscripted segment of his address: "I feel compelled to personally take on all the evil which some priests, quite a few in number [have committed] . . . to personally ask for forgiveness for the damage they have done for having sexually abused children. The Church is aware of this damage, it is personal, moral damage carried out by men of the Church, and we will not take one step backward with regards to how we will deal with this problem, and the sanctions that must be imposed. On the contrary, we have to be even stronger. Because you cannot interfere with children."

Clearly, the lesson here for businesspeople and leaders of all stripes is that serious matters require serious—and *timely*—action. Bergoglio's ability to overcome adversity in his youth sculpted him into a great leader; his unfortunate decision to try to sidestep adversity in this case has cast a small shadow of doubt on that greatness. Francis's actions of setting up a task force to deal with the abuses and his pleas for forgiveness, however, both show that he has learned from his fault of trying to sidestep the issue of sexual abuse in the Catholic Church. Only by acknowledging the problem can one begin to create steps to overcome it. In the case of the abuses of the Catholic Church, there is a very long road ahead. Yet Francis's change in attitude on the subject is an encouraging start.

The only way to meet challenges and hardships is head-on. Any attempt to step out of the way of problems merely allows them to snowball. As a result of Francis's failure to move faster to institute specific protocols and punishments when dealing with scandals, the press lambasted the Vatican and Pope Francis as well. Worse still, it allowed abuse victims and other marginalized members of the Church to feel forgotten—if not reviled—by their own attackers. One careless comment almost cost Francis so much of the hard work he had put into bringing strength back to the Church.

Don't make the same mistake Francis did. If you have a problem in your organization, whether it is a product, a service, or a member of senior management who violates the rules, it is incumbent upon you, as an effective leader, to deal with the worst first. As Peter Drucker put it, "[L]eadership is a foul-weather job." Make sure you have more than a cheap umbrella on hand when troubles start to rain down on your organization.

What other lessons can we apply from the Pope Francis example? Take a look at these ideas:

- *Turn Adversity into an Asset:* Adversity can be a positive thing, as long as you make it one. Adversity can help you make sure that you and your management team are not complacent.

(Recall Intel's Andy Grove and his concept of the strategic inflection point, from Chapter 7.) It is incumbent upon you and your colleagues to be trained to sniff out any significant change that has the ability to diminish or make your product offerings less valuable. In the event that you or another member of your team anticipates change before it sweeps across your industry, let everyone know what is happening and make sure that you and your colleagues make it a top priority.

- *Sidestepping Adversity Seldom Works:* Francis learned this lesson the hard way. Adversity is something that needs to be tackled head-on. By sweeping a problem under the rug, you are doing a disservice to yourself and, more important, your organization. Consider GM's recent failure to issue a timely recall of vehicles for having faulty ignition switches—a tragic move that allegedly cost at least ten people their lives. The move to delay the recall may have initially saved GM some money, but in the long run it has cost them an unquantifiable amount in the loss of consumer trust.

- *Be Proactive in Rooting Out Problems:* Consider putting together a small task force with the sole charter of discerning adverse issues and realities that could hurt your firm. You do not need to be a part of this task force. In fact, this group of employees should be closest to the customers and markets you serve. It is often the people on the front lines who get the first whiff of a problem or a competitor's move that might make one of your offerings obsolete.

CHAPTER 12

Pay Attention to Noncustomers

Pope Francis's ultimate goal is to personally reach as many of his flock as possible, and he wants all church leaders and members of the clergy to do the same. He wants to bring people closer to God regardless of religion, race, and sexual preference. Your goal in the world of business should be analogous. You must reach out to the outsiders—your noncustomers—to be successful.

Peter Drucker called potential customers *noncustomers*. It was Drucker who said that 90 percent of the information gathered by any institution comes from *inside* that organization. That is where most organizations get it wrong, explained Drucker; they need to look outside—for example, to the marketplace—where the most important things happen.

Drucker explained, "Increasingly, a winning strategy will require information about events and conditions outside the institution: non-customers, technologies other than those that are currently used by the company and present competitors, markets not currently served, and so on."

Once again there is a meeting of the minds between Pope Francis and the late Peter Drucker. These two thinkers also agree on ways of detecting real change: Francis talks about change in the way people feel about their religion, spirituality, God, and the Church, and for Drucker it is about how managers detect change that might make their "theories of the business obsolete."

Drucker has written much about the importance of describing one's customers; however, in his forty-plus books, and in other venues, he has also spoken of the importance of noncustomers. "The first signs of fundamental change rarely appear within one's own organization or among one's customers," he said. Instead, it is the people who are *not* buying your products or services who will "almost always" expose the changes that will soon affect your own institutions in profound ways.

⬥ POPE FRANCIS THE DRUCKER WAY

Francis does not see the world as a static place but as an ever-changing landscape that we all need to be attuned to. Here, Francis evokes shades of Drucker when he discusses a pastoral ministry. "Pastoral ministry in a missionary key seeks to abandon the complacent attitude that says: 'We have always done it that way.' I invite everyone to be bold and creative in this task of rethinking the goals, structures, style, and methods of evangelization in their respective communities. A proposal of goals without an adequate communal search for the means of achieving them will inevitably prove illusory."

Both Drucker and Francis are exceptional strategic thinkers. Pope Francis explains in his most noteworthy homily, *Evangelii Gaudium,* why a church must appeal to new members if it is going to succeed in its mission. "A Church which 'goes forth' is a Church whose doors are open. Going out to others in order to reach the fringes of humanity does not mean rushing out aimlessly into the world. Often it is better to slow down, to put aside our eagerness in order to see and listen to others, to stop rushing from one thing to another and to remain with someone who has faltered along the way. At times we have to be like the father of the prodigal son, who always keeps his door open so that when the son returns, he can readily pass through it."

He later elaborated, "We are aware of the importance of witnessing in our societies to that primordial openness to transcendence which lie[s] deep within the human heart. In this, we also sense our closeness to all those men and women who, although not identifying themselves as followers of any religious tradition, are nonetheless searching for truth, goodness, and beauty of God."

✤ REACHING CUSTOMERS AND NONCUSTOMERS

Let's take a step back to see how Francis has sharply increased the Church's "customer base." The United Kingdom's *MailOnline* published an article in November 2013, eight months after Bergoglio became Francis, with the headline "The Pope Effect: New Pontiff Has Seen Huge Increases in Church Congregations Since Election Eight Months Ago." The article states that cathedral attendance in the United Kingdom was up 20 percent since Francis's election, and that France, Spain, Italy, the United States, and Latin America all reported similar increases. Most noteworthy is that papal audiences are reported to draw crowds of eighty-five thousand people to Saint Peter's Square. To put that number in perspective, under Benedict XVI average attendance at the pope's weekly address was five thousand.

The article continues: "The 'Pope Francis Effect' is being felt across the world, with new and lapsed Catholics surging back to the confession box 'by the hundreds or thousands,' according to the Italian Center for Studies of New Religions." So what was the cause for all of this sudden renewed interest in Catholicism? The article credits Francis's "inspirational humility."

Yet Francis's humility only partly explains how he has successfully increased his "market share" in such dramatic fashion. One of the tools he has used to bring people back to church is the Internet and social media. With an astronomical 3.8 million Twitter followers, Francis can be called the first "digital pope." The numbers do not tell the whole story; it's the way Francis has used social media.

Starting in the summer of 2013, Francis used Twitter to offer "indulgences," which give Catholics a chance to lessen the amount of time they have to spend in purgatory. These "remissions" garnered a bad name in the Middle Ages because unscrupulous men would sell them for a small king's ransom. But Francis has turned that around.

At least one member of the Vatican "warned web-surfing Catholics that indulgences still required a dose of old-fashioned faith, and that paradise was not just a few mouse clicks away." One can imagine how more conservative members of the Vatican feel about Francis's new method for granting forgiveness. "You can't obtain indulgences like getting a coffee from a vending machine," Archbishop Claudio Maria Celli, head of the pontifical council for social communication, told the Italian daily *Corriere della Sera*."

Indulgences are given to believers who perform certain acts, such as scaling the Sacred Steps, which would allow a person to literally walk in the footsteps of Christ. For that single act, believers get to shave seven years off their time in purgatory. Believers can also win indulgences at certain key events and celebrations, such as the Catholic World Youth Day that takes place every summer in Rio de Janeiro.

Indulgences via the Web increase the Catholic Church's customer base. Those who were previously unable to make such pilgrimages can now communicate directly with the pope in ways they never could before. Following the pope's live tweets is now considered by the Church to be attendance at these sacred events.

The Internet also offers new measures to quantify the so-called Francis Effect. In 2013, Pope Francis was the most-discussed topic on the Internet, beating out such famous (and infamous) figures as Kate Middleton and Edward Snowden.

✧ DON'T FORGET ABOUT EXISTING CUSTOMERS

One more idea that Peter Drucker and Pope Francis have in common is making sure that when searching for new customers you don't neglect existing ones. "There is only one valid definition of a business purpose: to create a customer," declared Drucker. He added, however, that one of the most difficult tasks of any manager is defining his or her business.

Pope Francis understands intuitively how important it is to pay close attention to his existing flock. He said, "The preacher also needs to keep his ear to the people and to discover what it is that the faithful need to hear. A preacher has to contemplate the word, but he also has to contemplate his people. In this way he learns 'of the aspirations, of the riches and limitations, of ways of praying, of loving, of looking at the world, which distinguish this or that human gathering,' while paying attention 'to actual people, to using their language, their signs and symbols, to answering the questions they ask.'"

What steps can you take to get you closer to both customers and noncustomers? Consider the following items:

- *Seek Wisdom from Your Customers:* In this day and age, it is far more difficult than ever to hold on to key customers; competition is usually too intense—and global, depending upon your industry. Invite a select few of your largest customers to speak to your colleagues. By having top management from your key customers give a talk to your people to describe their greatest needs and problems, you solidify your relationship in a unique and progressive way. Before coming in, ask the customer to include a few words on "just what it is that keeps them up at night." This has the added benefit of giving meaning to your people's jobs. They will see how their work helps another and is appreciated.

- *Go to Your Noncustomers:* You will always have more noncustomers than customers, but so long as you know who your potential customers are, you can seek them out. Go to meetings, industry events, conventions, and anywhere else they gather. In addition, make a habit of reading the same newspapers and journals that these folks read. This puts you, literally, on the same page with them, and it might trigger ideas for new ways to increase your customer base.

- *Use Social Media:* Technology offers many ways to reach new customers as well. Choose which social media outlets appeal to your style of business (e.g., if you are in a creative industry, try Pinterest; if you are in a more corporate sphere, you might find many potential customers on LinkedIn). Join their conversations and give them something to talk about, even if it's not specifically your product. In addition, in this new world in which social media is so pervasive, there is no excuse not to have a website. If you have one, make sure you keep it current by blogging often. Give noncustomers a reason to come back to your site on a regular basis. If you do not have one, then it is time to go out and find a reputable firm to help you develop one. If Francis and his Vatican colleagues can use Twitter to keep people informed, there is little reason for you not to follow in his footsteps.

Source Notes

PROLOGUE

ix "Just as the commandment . . ." Pope Francis, *Evangelii Gaudium* ("The Joy of the Gospel"), apostolic exhortation, December 13, 2013.

ix "I'll stay down here." Chelsea J. Carter, Ada Messia, and Richard Allen Greene, "Pope Francis, the Pontiff of Firsts, Breaks with Tradition," CNN, March 14, 2013. http://www.cnn.com/2013/03/13/world/europe/vatican-pope-selection/.

x "He was not an ingénue . . ." Jason Horowitz and Jim Yardley, "Pope with the Humble Touch Is Firm in Reshaping the Vatican," *New York Times,* January 13, 2014.

x "Bergoglio has shown himself . . ." Mark Binelli, "Pope Francis: The Times They Are A-Changin'," *Rolling Stone,* January 28, 2014.

x "building bridges among . . ." Jorge Mario Bergoglio and Abraham Skorka, *On Heaven and Earth* (New York: Image/Random House, 2013).

xi "How can it be that it is not a news item . . ." Pope Francis, *Evangelii Gaudium.*

xi "Possess no gold or silver . . ." Luke 9:1–3.

xii "The economy can no longer . . ." Pope Francis, *Evangelii Gaudium.*

xii "Business is a vocation . . ." Ibid.

xii "A new tyranny is thus born . . ." Ibid.

xiv "Let us never forget . . ." Pope Francis, Mass, Imposition of the Pallium and Bestowal of the Fisherman's Ring for the Beginning of the Petrine Ministry of the Bishop of Rome, homily, March 19, 2013.

xv "Any society needs institutions . . ." Peter Drucker, *Concept of the Corporation* (1946; repr. Piscataway, NJ: Transaction Publishers, 1993), 117.

xv "If a social institution operates . . ." Ibid.

xv "It is vital that government leaders . . ." Pope Francis, *Evangelii Gaudium.*

xv "Changing structures without generating . . ." Ibid.

xv "It is hard to fight them . . ." Peter Drucker, *Managing in a Time of Great Change* (New York: Dutton, 1995), 41–42.

xv "The renewal of structures . . ." Pope Francis, *Evangelii Gaudium.*

xvi "I ask you to ensure humanity . . ." Pope Francis, Statement to World Economic Forum, January 21, 2014.

xvi "Some people continue to defend . . ." *Evangelii Gaudium.*

xvi "[a] religious who recognizes . . ." Ibid.

INTRODUCTION: FROM BERGOGLIO TO FRANCIS

1   "92 percent of Catholics . . ." Gary Larder, "Pope Francis, *Time* Magazine's Person of the Year, Is Vastly Popular Among Catholics," *ABC News*, December 11, 2013.

2   "beautifully written . . ." Ibid.

4   "As a young man . . ." Chris Lowney, *Pope Francis: Why He Leads the Way He Leads—Lessons from the First Jesuit Pope* (Chicago, Loyola Press, 2013), 34.

4   In March 1958 . . . Ibid., 16.

5   During the coming years Ibid., 53–54.

5   "No. I did not want to be pope . . ." Ibid., 13.

6   "In December 2011 . . . he submitted . . ." Ibid., 58.

CHAPTER 1: LEAD WITH HUMILITY

7 "we have scores of books . . ." John Dame and Jeffrey Gedmin, "Six Principles for Developing Humility as a Leader," *HBR Blog Network*, September 9, 2013.

7 "If we can develop a truly humble . . ." Bergoglio and Skorka, *On Heaven and Earth*, 229.

8 "In the prevailing culture . . ." Pope Francis, *Evangelii Gaudium*.

8 "We have to be humble . . ." Pope Francis, quoted in "Be Humble 'from Head to Toe,' Pope Francis Says," *Catholic News Agency*, June 14, 2013. http://www.catholicnewsagency.com/news/be-humble-from-head-to-toe-pope-francis-says/.

8 "His humility is already becoming legendary . . ." "A Man of Firsts, Pope Francis Is Remarkably Humble and Conservative," *Catholic Online*, March 14, 2013.

9 "As I am a believer, I know . . ." Bergoglio and Skorka, *On Heaven and Earth*, 12–13.

9 " 'If the CEO's goal . . ." Helen Coster, "CEOs Who Work in Cubicles," *Forbes*, June 9, 2010.

9 Former eBay CEO Meg Whitman . . . Ibid.

11 "Let us never forget that authentic . . ." Pope Francis, Mass, Imposition of the Pallium.

11 "Christians are called to do . . ." Pope Francis, *Evangelii Gaudium*.

12 "Jesus says that the one . . ." Bergoglio and Skorka, *On Heaven and Earth*, 230.

12 "Dialogue is born from . . ." Ibid., xvi.

13 "There are many barriers . . ." Ibid., xiv–xv.

CHAPTER 2: SMELL LIKE YOUR FLOCK

15 "smell like your flock . . ." Pope Francis, first Chrism Mass, March 28, 2013.

15 **"made an assistant bishop . . ."** Paul Vallely, *Pope Francis: Untying the Knots* (London: Bloomsbury, 2013), xi.

16 *Paco*—**a cheap and dangerous form** . . . Ibid., 98.

16 **"*parroquia* (the parish) looked . . ."** Ibid.

16 **Padre Pepe contacted Bergoglio** . . . Ibid., 99.

16 **"The day after Pepe was threatened . . ."** Ibid.

17 **The "Bishop of the Slums" even volunteered** . . . Ibid.

17 **"those that had been tossed . . ."** Ibid., 100.

18 **"I'm Congressman Horsford."** "Steven Horsford, Nevada Congressman, Goes 'Undercover' with UPS," Associated Press, February 23, 2014.

20 **"TWIST reinforces our values . . ."** "Tesco Week in Store Together," http://www.tesco-careers.com/home/working/training-and -development/twist.

20 **"It's difficult to completely evade . . ."** Michael Trimmer, "The Francis Effect," *Christian Today*, November 13, 2013.

▓ CHAPTER 3: WHO AM I TO JUDGE?

23 **"[A] lobby of the greedy . . ."** Binelli, "Pope Francis: The Times They Are A-Changin'."

23 **"A gay person who is seeking God . . ."** Ibid.

23 **"Could five little words . . ."** Tracy Connor, "'Who Am I to Judge?': The Pope's Most Powerful Phrase in 2013," *NBC News*, December 22, 2013.

24 **"In Buenos Aires I used to . . ."** Pope Francis, "A Big Heart Open to God," interview by Antonio Spadaro, *La Civiltà Cattolica*, *America*, August 9, 2013.

25 **"Dialog must be serious . . ."** Ibid.

25 **"Today more than ever we need . . ."** Pope Francis, *Evangelii Gaudium*.

26 "when I entrust something . . ." Ibid.

26 "He [Pope Francis] sat with them . . ." Michael Sean Winters and Massimo Franco, "Survival," *National Catholic Reporter*, December 2013–January 2014.

26 "There is a striking difference . . ." Ibid.

26 "My authoritarian and quick manner . . ." Pope Francis, "A Big Heart Open to God."

27 "I did not always do . . ." Winters and Franco, "Survival."

27 "It was a novel move . . ." Massimo Franco, "The Possible Revolution of Pope Francis," *Survival*, December 2013–January 2014.

28 "One of the most serious temptations . . ." Pope Francis, *Evangelii Gaudium*.

28 "The sixteen behaviors (competencies) . . ." John Senger and Joseph Folkman, *The Extraordinary Leader: Turning Good Managers into Great Leaders* (New York: McGraw-Hill, 2009), 102–108.

29 "We have to regard ourselves as sealed . . ." Pope Francis, *Evangelii Gaudium*.

CHAPTER 4: DON'T CHANGE—REINVENT

31 "to regularize different situations . . ." Pope Francis, "Bergoglio Talks About His Revolutionary First Year at the Head of the Church," interview by Ferruccio de Bortoli, *Corriere della Sera*, March 5, 2013.

31 "Pope Francis celebrated Mass . . ." *Vatican Radio*, February 28, 2014.

32 "intelligent, courageous and full of love . . ." Pope Francis, quoted by Andrea Tornielli, "Francis Calls for 'Intelligent' and 'Courageous' Pastoral Approach to the Family," *Vatican Insider*, February 21, 2014.

33 Regardless of his intentions . . . James Carroll, "Who Am I to Judge?," *The New Yorker*, December 23, 2013.

35 "a sinner who God in his mercy . . ." Vallely, *Pope Francis: Untying the Knots*, 94.

36 "In the final days, as Congregations . . ." Ibid., 155.

36 "The only purpose of the Church . . ." Ibid.

36 "The next Pope should be someone . . ." Ibid.

37 "Bergoglio was the first man . . ." Ibid.

37 "There was a new pope . . ." Ibid.

37 *"Acceptasne electionem de te . . ."* Ibid.

38 "Francis I, the first Jesuit Pope . . ." Massimo Franco, "The First Global Pope," *Survival*, June–July 2013.

CHAPTER 5: MAKE INCLUSION A TOP PRIORITY

42 "small chapel focused on doctrine . . ." Laurie Goodstein, "Pope Bluntly Faults Church's Focus on Gays and Abortion," *Sydney Morning Herald*, September 20, 2013.

43 "the first reform must be the attitude . . ." Pope Francis, "A Big Heart Open to God."

43 "Dialogue entails a warm reception . . ." Bergoglio and Skorka, *On Heaven and Earth*, xiv–xv.

44 "There are many barriers . . ." Ibid.

44 "You will not stay behind . . ." Andres Gagliarducci, "Pope Francis Tells Almoner to Make It Personal in Charities Office Reform," *National Catholic Register*, October 17, 2013.

45 "Instead of being just a church . . ." Pope Francis, "A Big Heart Open to God."

46 "I can see clearly . . ." Antonio Spadaro, "A Big Heart Open to God," *America: The National Catholic Review*, September 30, 2013.

46 "It was a novel move . . ." Franco, "The Possible Revolution of Pope Francis."

CHAPTER 6: AVOID INSULARITY

50 *"[NIH] is the philosophy . . ."* Nicholas J. Webb and Chris Thoen, *The Innovation Playbook: A Revolution in Business Excellence* (Hoboken, NJ: John Wiley & Sons, 2010), 83.

52 "With Pope Francis a new phase . . ." Annemarie C. Mayer, "Pope Francis: A Pastor According to the Heart of Christ," *International Journal for the Study of the Christian Church*, May 23, 2013.

53 "When someone is self-sufficient . . ." Bergoglio and Skorka, *On Heaven and Earth*, 12–13.

53 "The great leaders of the people . . ." Ibid., 32.

54 "I know more agnostic people . . ." Ibid., 13.

55 "And now I would like to give . . ." Pope Francis, Apostolic Blessing "Urbi et Orbi," First Greeting of the Holy Father Pope Francis, March 13, 2013.

55 "Any religious leader that is prideful . . ." Bergoglio and Skorka, *On Heaven and Earth*, 31.

56 "Those who stubbornly try to recover . . ." Pope Francis, "A Big Heart Open to God."

CHAPTER 7: CHOOSE PRAGMATISM OVER IDEOLOGY

58 "I don't have all the answers . . ." Vallely, *Pope Francis: Untying the Knots*, 131.

58 "I do not have any doubt . . ." Bergoglio and Skorka, *On Heaven and Earth*, 23.

59 "Here I repeat . . ." Pope Francis, *Evangelii Gaudium*.

59 "I admit that the tempo . . ." Bergoglio and Skorka, *On Heaven and Earth*, 26.

60 "If the Christian . . . wants everything . . ." Pope Francis, "A Big Heart Open to God."

62 "The frontiers are many." Ibid.

62 "Certainly Bergoglio in all phases . . ." Vallely, *Pope Francis: Untying the Knots*, 143.

CHAPTER 8: EMPLOY THE OPTICS OF DECISION MAKING

65 "We are all Political animals . . ." Bergoglio and Skorka, *On Heaven and Earth*, 136.

66 "Something has happened to our politics . . ." Ibid., 140–141.

67 it was also noteworthy . . . Michael Terheyden, "Pope Francis Offers the World an Example of True Leadership," *Catholic Online*, March 25, 2013.

67 "It is clear that his decision . . ." Vallely, *Pope Francis: Untying the Knots*, 143.

68 "I am always wary . . ." Pope Francis, "A Big Heart Open to God."

68 "Good people–judgment calls . . ." Noel Tichy and Warren Bennis, *Judgment: How Winning Leaders Make Great Calls* (New York: Penguin, 2007).

68 When Michael Eisner nabbed . . . Michael Wolff, "Eisner Un-Moused?," *New York Magazine*, July 12, 1999.

69 "In a small world such as the Vatican . . ." John Allen, "Francis Reboots Vatican System with New Secretary of State," *National Catholic Reporter*, August 31, 2013.

69 Francis revealed in an interview . . . Franco, "The Possible Revolution of Pope Francis."

70 Pope Francis offered Parolin . . . Joshua J. McElwee, "New Vatican Secretary of State Says Change Will Come to His Office," *National Catholic Reporter*, December 4, 2013.

70 "Parolin's temperament suggests . . ." Gianni Valenti, "The Talents of the Priest and Diplomat Fr. Pietro Parolin," *Vatican Insider*, August 30, 2013.

70 "It may be Francis's nomination . . ." Franco, "The Possible Revolution of Pope Francis."

71 "Bertone has been accused . . ." Alessandro Speciale, "Pope Francis Taps Diplomat Pietro Parolin as Vatican's New 'Prime Minister,'" Religion News Service, August 31, 2013.

72 "Above all, I feel the full weight . . ." "Pope Francis Appoints New Vatican Secretary of State," *Catholic Herald*, August 31, 2013.

72 "I really hope there will be . . ." McElwee, "New Vatican Secretary of State Says Change Will Come to His Office."

CHAPTER 9: RUN YOUR ORGANIZATION LIKE A FIELD HOSPITAL

74 "The thing the church needs . . ." Pope Francis, "A Big Heart Open to God."

76 "How are we treating the people . . ." Ibid.

76 "We must form their hearts . . ." Ibid.

78 "Countless issues involving . . ." Pope Francis, *Evangelii Gaudium*.

78 "The teacher who nullifies . . ." Bergoglio and Skorka, *On Heaven and Earth*, 70.

CHAPTER 10: LIVE ON THE FRONTIER

81 "The sister lived on the frontier . . ." Pope Francis, "A Big Heart Open to God."

82 "Wake up the world!" Antonio Spadaro, "Wake up the World: Conversation with Pope Francis about the Religious Life," *La Civiltà Cattolica*, Revised January 6, 2014.

82 "When it comes to social issues . . ." Pope Francis, "A Big Heart Open to God."

83 "need to become acquainted with reality . . ." Spadaro, "Wake Up the World."

CHAPTER 11: CONFRONT ADVERSITY HEAD-ON

89 "Jorge Mario Bergoglio is a doctrinal . . ." Vallely, *Pope Francis: Untying the Knots,* xi.

90 "She taught me the seriousness . . ." Ibid., 24.

91 "When a priest abuses . . ." Ibid., 12.

91 "The Catholic Church is perhaps . . ." Clyde Haberman, "The Fight to Reveal Abuses by Catholic Priests," *New York Times,* March 30, 2014.

91 "To some ears, those remarks . . ." Ibid.

92 The makeup of the commission . . . Steve Scherer, "Pope Appoints Former Child Victim to Church Group on Sex Abuse," Reuters, March 22, 2014. http://www.reuters.com/article/2014/03/22/us-pope-abuse-commission-idUSBREA2L0D520140322.

92 "I feel compelled to personally take on . . ." Pope Francis, "Pope Francis on Clerical Sexual Abuse: Not One Step Back," Vatican Radio, April 11, 2014. http://en.radiovaticana.va/news/2014/04/11/pope_francis_on_clerical_sexual_abuse:_not_one_step_back/en1-789927.

93 "[L]eadership is a foul-weather job" Peter Drucker, *The Nonprofit Organization* (1992; repr. New York: HarperBusiness, 2006).

CHAPTER 12: PAY ATTENTION TO NONCUSTOMERS

95 "Increasingly, a winning strategy . . ." Peter Drucker, quoted in Robert A. Paton and James McCalman, *Change Management: A Guide to Effective Implementation,* 3rd ed. (London: Sage Publications, 2000).

96 "The first signs of fundamental . . ." Ibid.

96 "Pastoral ministry in a missionary . . ." Pope Francis, *Evangelii Gaudium.*

96 "A Church which 'goes forth' . . ." Ibid.

97 "We are aware of the importance . . ." Pope Francis, Address of the Holy Father Pope Francis, March 20, 2013.

97 The United Kingdom's *MailOnline* . . . Ellie Buchdahl, "The Pope Effect: New Pontiff Has Seen Huge Increases in Church Congregations Since Election Eight Months Ago," *MailOnline*, November 17, 2013.

97 "The 'Pope Francis Effect' . . ." Ibid.

98 "You can't obtain indulgences like getting a coffee . . ." Archbishop Claudio Maria Celli, interview by *Corriere della Sera*, quoted in Tom Kington, "Vatican Offers 'Time Off Purgatory' to Followers of Pope Francis Tweets," *The Guardian*, July 16, 2013.

98 Indulgences are given . . . Ibid.

99 "There is only one valid definition . . ." Peter Drucker, *The Practice of Management* (1954, repr. New York: HarperBusiness, 2006).

99 "The preacher also needs to keep . . ." Pope Francis, *Evangelii Gaudium*.

Acknowledgments

There are a number of people to whom I would like to offer my heartfelt thanks—and without whom this book may never have happened.

I start with my foundation, my family, who give me more support than one man deserves.

To my wife, Nancy, who loved the idea the instant she heard it. And who always has amazing ideas for turning the good into great.

To Joshua and Noah, my beautiful and brilliant boys, who selflessly shared their time with me, and Pope Francis, in the most generous way they knew how.

To my dad, the hero of my life, who gave me the inspiration and the wisdom to discern the inspiration and wisdom of Pope Francis. My dad, Barton "Baruch" Krames, will turn 87 years of age by the time of this book's publication. An incredible feat for someone who expected to perish before his sixteenth birthday.

And to my late mother, Trudy Krames, who allowed me to recognize the unprecedented humanity in Pope Francis. My mom knew a great deal about humility, and I can only hope that a bit of it rubbed off on me.

I want to thank several publishing professionals as well, without whom this book may never have lived up to my own strict standards. The folks at AMACOM deserve a double entry here. First, they put up with me in the early going when I gave in to the "non-Francis" parts of my personality. Next, they brought nothing but professionalism to the project at every turn, displaying their incredibly sharp publishing instincts at every turn. They were the first, and fastest, to offer me a publishing contract, and for that I am eternally grateful.

The two individuals who deserve much of the praise are Stephen S. Power, my editor, and Ellen Kadin, who knew right when to step in and talk me off the ledge on which I had put myself on more than one occasion. It was Stephen who pulled together a superb team to work on the book even though my behavior did not warrant it. Like the subject of this book, I, too, am a sinner who made it this far only through the grace and forgiveness of God.

And my heartfelt gratitude to my venerable, long-standing mentor, Hank Kennedy, who made me an editor in 1984 and three decades later stepped out of the arena after showing me great generosity by acquiring me and this book. That was a grand gesture, but for Hank, just one of thousands he made in a remarkable career that spanned nearly half a century.

For her copyediting virtuosity, I would like to single out the ever-so-talented Ginny Carroll. Ginny is the best in the business and treats every book—and author—with great care and thoughtfulness.

I would like to offer my heartfelt thanks to Rocco Ortenzio, a model of humility, for reading the manuscript and offering some superb suggestions. As always, I owe him a debt of gratitude.

I also thank Ellen Kokontis and Kelli Christiansen for helping me with the researching and editing of the book. Their contributions are appreciated more than they know.

There were several others who played a role in helping me to turn a good idea into the book that materialized in the nights and very early mornings that it took to get this book into print. I offer my warm thanks to Bernadette Berarardi Coletta, who helped me to navigate the depth of spirit to understand the nuances of Pope Francis. And also a warm thanks to my supporters Mark Walker and

Bezalel Dantz for helping to keep me grounded. They helped from afar on those toughest middle-of-the-night writing sessions when sleep was hard to come by.

And thanks also to my eternal childhood friend, Billy Budd, to whom I still owe a martini the next time I fly into New York. He was a true friend as a child, and now, four decades later, remains as true as he did when we played together on Sedgwick Avenue, the schoolyard, and other streets in our diverse Bronx neighborhood.

And last, how could I possibly conclude this book without thanking Jorge Mario Bergoglio—Pope Francis—who helped me to see the world in a new light. He might be a sinner, but he is a sinner who has brought an eternal light and limitless joy to a world that was in dire need of both. He is simply the most authentic leader I have ever had the good fortune to observe.

—Jeffrey A. Krames
April 2014

Index

accessibility
  of business leaders, 12, 13–14,
    21, 79
  to customers, 98–99
adversity
  faced by Bergoglio, 88–90
  faced by business leaders, 90–94
agnosticism, 54
Allen, John, 69
ambition
  of Bergoglio, 33–35, 39, 84
  vs. humility, 84–86
Apple Computer, 4, 21, 61
Argentine Episcopal Conference, 6
assessments
  of decisions made, 68, 73
  of performance, 25, 27–30
atheism, 9, 54

Beatles, 28
Benedict XVI (pope), 1, 6, 33–35, 39,
    61, 71, 97
Bennis, Warren, 68
Bergoglio, Jorge Mario. *See also*
    Francis I (pope)
  at 2013 conclave, 36–37, 63, 84
  ambitions of, 33–35, 39, 84
  authoritarianism of, x, 26–27, 67, 78
  background of, 4–6, 88–90
  as Bishop of the Slums, 15–17, 41
  courage of, 62

humility of, ix
  tolerance shown by, 24
Bertone, Cardinal Tarcisio, 71
best practices
  improving on, 56
  sharing, 57
Binelli, Mark, x
BlackBerry, 61, 76–77
"bling bishop." *See* Tebartz-van Elst,
    Bishop Franz-Peter
Bloomberg, Michael, 10
Bortoli, Ferruccio de, 31
Brin, Sergey, 10
Buenos Aires
  Bergoglio as bishop of, 5–6
  drug war in, 15–17
bureaucracy
  of Catholic Church, 71, 81
  streamlining, 39–40
Bush, George W., 45
business organizations
  ambition in, 83–87
  confronting problems in, 63,
    93–94
  decision making in, 66, 68–69,
    72–73
  field hospital analogy for, 76–77
  inclusiveness in, 46–49
  insularity in, 55–57
  lean, 47
  making assessments in, 24–30

119

About the Author

JEFFREY A. KRAMES (Chicago, IL) is the author of the *New York Times* bestsellers *The Welch Way* and *The Rumsfeld Way*, as well as many other leadership books. He has been published in *The New York Times, The Wall Street Journal, Barron's, Financial Times,* and other leading publications, and has been interviewed by Fox News, CNBC, MSNBC, CNN, A&E's *Biography,* the BBC, among other major media outlets.

* 9 7 8 1 4 0 0 2 4 5 5 8 1 *